What the experts are saying about this book:

Craig Boddington
Editor, **Petersen's Hunting** wrote:

*"*A buddy of mine likes to say, 'We need more hunters writing and fewer writers hunting,' meaning that, unfortunately, all too many folks in my business hunt better with their word processors than with their legs, binoculars, and rifles. This does not apply to Lance Stapleton. He's a good storyteller besides.

In this book he sets a daunting goal for himself, to take exceptional bucks of fully six varieties of North American deer: whitetail, Coues' whitetail, blacktail, Sitka blacktail, Rocky Mountain mule deer, and desert mule deer. I have some concept of how difficult a task this would be. I have hunted all of these deer and, many years ago, I set a similar goal for myself. Except, back then, we didn't consider either Sitka blacktails or desert mule deer separately. So my 'deer grand slam' was comprised of just four varieties…and at the conclusion I was exhausted and didn't ever want to try it again! Lance's marathon season thus included not only more deer, but he also set higher standards for himself. It was a long journey, but a uniquely successful one.

You will enjoy it from the comfort of your easy chair, but you'll share the excitement and the heartache, and you'll almost certainly learn a few things from a fine writer and truly great deer hunter as he shares his ultimate deer hunting quest.*"*

J. Scott Olmsted
Executive Editor of **American Hunter**

"It's no stretch to suggest the deer as the centerpiece of a hunter's heart. It's quite another thing entirely to bag all six subspecies of the critter in a single year. Yet when I met Lance Stapleton he was doing just that.

"'A 'triple-double?'" I asked. "In one year? Huh. Hadn't thought of that before. And you're gonna write a book about it?"

Indeed, in the midst of my own career such a feat isn't fathomable. But Lance retired recently, then chased his dream seasons across the continent. Naturally, I'm envious. More than that, as a reader and a witness to part of his "Deer Quest" I'm curious.

I couldn't resist the read. Beyond the expected recollections of the hunts themselves in Stapleton's work lies respect for the deer only those of us afield can understand, splendid scenery, and new friends young and old to cement so many new memories. Sounds like a great way to spend a couple months, if you've got the time.

Like I said: I'm envious. But I'm not jealous. I'll chase my own dream seasons when I retire. Until then I have this journal to savor."

John H. Roush, Jr.
Worldwide hunter and **author** wrote:

"The stories in this fabulous collection ring true, for I have hunted nearby locations for the same species. The difficulty of bagging any buck of the six varieties he hunted that would meet the tremendously difficult standards for B&C is well known. For one to collect such fine trophies of all six species in one Fall season seems to me an insurmountable goal. These fascinating stories are testament to a tremendously capable hunter—I know, for I have hunted with him."

Bob Robb

Editor of **Bowmasters** magazine and columnist for **North American Hunter** magazine commented:

"When it comes to deer hunting, Lance Stapleton is a 'been there, done that' kind of guy who has paid his dues in sweat equity for decades. In this book he shares stories of the hunt in the old style, without the know-it-all 'how-to' format so common—and so drab—found in most modern hunting magazines. Reading this book makes we want to lace up my boots, grab my favorite rifle, and head for the mountains, right now!"

Dwight Schuh

Editor of **Bowhunter Magazine**

"One thing is unquestionable—Lance Stapleton is a deer hunting nut. So it's not surprising when Lance celebrates his retirement by setting out to take six record book subspecies of deer in one season. Not all the rest of us deer nuts enjoy such a luxury, but we can enjoy the thrill vicariously as we follow Lance across North America. His first-person accounts of his Deer Quest are entertaining and educational—must reading for anyone who confesses to being a deer hunting nut."

Don Causey

President and Publisher of **The Hunting Report** said:

"Lance Stapleton knows as much about North American big game hunting as anyone I know. His in-depth knowledge of the subject, coupled with his passion for going afield and for setting near-impossible goals for himself, make this book must reading for the dedicated big game hunter."

Ken Nowicki

Senior Editor of **Big Game Adventure** commented:

"The greatest hunting stories from yesteryear were just that—Stories of the Hunt. Good writing will capture the thrills and spills and the imagination. Stapleton also captures the 'hard work' that a hunt entails. There are long days and cold nights and day after day and week after week expended looking for good trophies and hitting his personal standard. This book details a year of prime adventure. As with his hunting, Stapleton seeks the high standard with his writing and his diverse experience and his professional style makes his quest for a "triple double" a pleasure to read. I highly recommend it. Deer hunters and anyone who appreciates good outdoor writing will want this book in their library."

German Rivas

Director and Editor of **Caza Mayor** wrote:

"This book is a masterpiece in our hunting literature because Lance Stapleton is an outstanding writer who keeps you reading page after page; but, besides that, this book has an enormous historical value, because the quest to kill that many deer in one year is something that had never been done before."

DEER *Quest*

In Search of a "Triple-Double" on Deer

by
**LANCE
STAPLETON**

OUTDOOR EXPERIENCES UNLIMITED
SALEM, OREGON

2 0 0 2

DEER QUEST
In Search of a "Triple-Double" on Deer
by Lance Stapleton

Library of Congress Cataloging-in-Publication Data
Stapleton, Lance
Deer Quest: In Search of a "Triple-Double" on Deer / by Lance Stapleton

Softcover Edition:
Library of Congress Control Number: 2002094826
ISBN 0-9634538-1-5 $19.95
Hardcover Edtion:
Library of Congress Control Number: 2002114585
ISBN 0-9634538-5-8 $24.95
Published by:
Outdoor Experiences Unlimited   Editors: Terry Sheely and Jane Loftus
PO Box 4126   Cover Montage: David Creech
Salem, Oregon 97302-8126   Book Design: Lydia Inglett Spears

Dedication

This book is dedicated to the guides, outfitters, and booking agents who helped me achieve a lifelong dream. Only after I finished my hunts did I truly appreciate the effort required from guides and outfitters who hunt every day of the season.

These guys pound the mountains, deserts, and prairies day-in and day-out and do it with a smile. They are the first up in the morning and the last to hit the sack. Along the way, they give a bit of themselves and willingly share knowledge earned while paying their dues in the field. And more importantly, they share our memories of mountains and plains, fresh air, wild game, and hunting experiences.

What more could you ask?

Foreword

A FEW YEARS AGO, a hunting buddy and I sat in deer camp, coffee cups in hand, ruminating out loud about the problems of the world, the deer-hunting world to be specific. It was a cold November Sunday, a non-deer hunting day by law, and with nothing to do but put in the hours until the next morning, we (as deer hunters are wont to do) attempted to solve these problems.

The truth be known, we didn't actually solve much that day; talk we did and drink too many pots of coffee we did, but "solve" I'm afraid we didn't do much of. At the end of the day, in spite of our best intentions, the most we'd accomplished was to define what we considered to be the one fundamental problem afflicting the glorious tradition of deer hunting, to whit: the lack of deer hunting "adventure" writings in the popular press. Both of us had grown up reading the deer hunting adventure stories of yore, stories of big bucks and hard hunts, stories of wild places and stalks both successful and failed, stories that inspired us and others like us to take to the field in search of our own adventures.

So what happened to those adventure stories and when did that "what" happen? Much as we tried that cold Sunday, we couldn't put a finger on the exact day the "adventure" era ended and the "how to" era began, sometime during the 1970s or so we figured. Perhaps the change was a gradual shift into the information age or perhaps the change was the brain child of some marketing "whiz bang," sitting in a big city corporate office somewhere, deciding that hunting adventure stories were passé and that deer hunters really needed ten million hardcore "how to" hunt deer articles and books.

Who knows for sure how, why and when it happened, the fact is, it did. For two decades, the last two, North American magazine racks and bookstore shelves have overflowed with variations on a single theme, the "Top 10" secrets to deer hunting success. Obviously hunters did need and want the information, because these "how to" stories sold. They sold so well in fact that a new breed of outdoor writer evolved, a writer who was better at researching and creating "how to" hunt deer articles than they were at actually hunting deer. Sitting there sipping on our coffee, my hunting buddy and I rued this reality, and pined for the day when the pendulum would swing back again, swing back to herald a new age of deer hunting adventure stories, stories that entertain, inform and inspire.

We may have pined, but we didn't hold our breath. It isn't an easy thing to do, writing adventure stories that is. It takes Olympian amounts of dedication and time...and effort. To write adventure stories, the author has to have a family that understands and is willing to sacrifice right along with the hunter\author and more importantly is willing to forgive that hunter\author's extended absences. No true adventure takes place at home in front of the word processor, adventure cannot be researched, it must be experienced where it happens, away from loved ones, in faraway cold places, hot places, windy, wet and wild places. And this means discipline and expense.

No, deer hunting adventure writing isn't an easy trail to cut and although my hunting partner and I determined what the problem was, we didn't solve it. Certainly I, as a writer thought about trying, but there was a limit to my desire. Deer are tough to hunt, the toughest to hunt in some cases and I for one wasn't willing to take the first step down that trail. Thankfully so, as it turns out, because another hunter, a true hunter by every definition, met the challenge far more adequately than I could have (though I despair to admit it.) That hunter didn't just take the first step, he took a giant leap! That hunter was Lance Stapleton and he has done what so badly needed to be done for the deer hunting world, he's written the book that will set the new standard by which all the new millennium's deer hunting books will be judged.

Lance traveled from the top to the bottom of this continent on a one-year deer-hunting odyssey, the adventure of a lifetime, a Deer Quest for the "triple-double," a goal that the rest of us less ambitious deer hunters could barely have imagined if not for Lance's writings. Even the thought of the effort involved, trying to kill one record book-sized deer of each of the six deer species boggles the mind! One or two in a lifetime of hunting? Sure, maybe, but all in one year? The goal in and of itself smacks of adventure and frankly, after two decades of "how to," I for one am ready for it!

Bring it on! Take me to Old Mexico hunting for the "Gray Ghosts" of the high desert, tell me hunting stories about Mossyhorn blacktails with the legendary Schaafsmas in the coastal mountains of Northern California, and talk to me about Sitka deer in the land of the Midnight Sun! I want it all, I want to hear about brown bears and mountains, buster bucks in Utah and Pilgrimages to El Carbon, I want to share the magic of Santa Rosa Island. I want adventure again!

Deer hunters want adventure again!

Thank you Lance for showing us the way.

—Jim Shockey
British Columbia, Canada

Contents

Foreword by Jim Shockey   *ix*

Preface   15

section one

Blacktail Deer   19

North America's Toughest Deer Trophy   21

Mossyhorns of Trinity County   29

Blacktail in the Land of the Midnight Sun   43

section two

Mule Deer   61

Nobody's Fool   63

Magic on Santa Rosa Island   73

Buster Bucks in Utah   91

Pilgrimage to El Carbon   105

Treasure of San José   117

section three

Whitetail Deer   137

The King   139

Whitetails in the Black Hills   151

Tough Hunts for Kansas Whitetails   163

Mexico's "Other" Whitetail   177

The Gray Ghost of Chihuahua   189

section four

Straight Talk   209

Gear and Services   211

section five

Appendix   227

Outfitters, Guides and the Like   229

The Last Word   233

About The Author   237

Order Form   239

Preface

A S I DROVE AWAY from my last day at work, my emotions were running wild. I was ecstatic because I had finally achieved a lifelong dream—early retirement! Still, before I drove away, I turned to look at the building where for years I had spent most of my waking hours and whispered simply, "Thank You, God!"

I had enjoyed my work, at least most of the time, but now I looked forward to major changes in almost every aspect of my life. The anticipation of the unknown was exhilarating, yet a little frightening. My wife and I had long prepared and sacrificed for this day. We had forgone the expensive toys that most of our neighbors felt were necessities: long vacations, expensive cars, second homes, and big boats. Instead, we had methodically prepared for our early retirement over the last four decades, and finally it was payday!

Our plan was in place, and we were moving rapidly toward our new lives. I had a slight head start on my wife, who elected to work several more months before retiring. This left a gap in our timetable, a lucky gap as it turned out.

Lying in bed, long after the lights were out, I often fantasized about deer hunting. I already had a collection of deer mounts over my fireplace, shot on memorable hunts scattered over almost five decades. A half-dozen times I had killed, in single hunting seasons, the so-called "grand slam" of deer: mule deer, whitetail, blacktail, and Coues deer.

To celebrate my retirement, I decided that I wanted to do something special, sort of a reward to myself for years of hard work. The thought struck me that there were actually six major deer species in

North America. It would be an incredible and difficult challenge to shoot all six bucks in one year. Perhaps that is why it had never been done.

Adopting another popular sports term, I decided to call my quest a "triple-double" of deer. Let me explain.

The triple part of my quest was the three major species of deer in North America: white-tailed, black-tailed, and mule deer. The double part comes from the fact that each of the three species is made up of two subspecies. White-tailed deer are divided into northern and Coues varieties; black-tailed deer include the Columbian and Sitka subspecies; and mule deer include the Rocky Mountain and the desert varieties.

In a moment of innocent bravado, I decided to make my quest even more difficult. I adopted the Boone and Crockett Club (B&C) Awards Program minimum typical scores as my target for each species, with one exception. Since B&C doesn't recognize the desert mule deer as a separate subspecies, I would use their minimum score of 180 points for both the Rocky Mountain and desert varieties.

To kill six record book-class bucks in one year was an awesome challenge, perhaps even bordering on impossible! Still, the hunts were to be a celebration of my retirement, and I didn't want the project to deteriorate into a win/lose contest. Early in the planning stages I decided to accept the gross scores of my bucks because I believe that a buck should get credit for every inch of antler it develops.

The final plan I settled upon was to kill six bucks with the highest total gross score I could achieve. The B&C Awards minimums became my goal because I respect how difficult it is to meet them. As another restriction, I would not hunt behind fences where killing a big whitetail could be a great deal easier than hunting open range lands.

Ignorance is bliss! Only when I started to put my plan into play did it dawn on me that the actual hunts weren't my biggest challenge. The real problem was logistically fitting that much hunting into a single season. My Deer Quest was, in fact, a scheduling nightmare. I originally thought that most hunts would take place in October and November. Instead, friends, guides, outfitters, and my booking agents convinced me that I should concentrate on hunting during special early season hunts, when the bucks are still in bachelor groups, or late seasons, when the bucks are in the rut. The early and late hunts gave me the best chance to look over as many deer as possible and to find bucks with racks that met my goals.

The bright spot was that a number of my outfitter friends were intrigued by the challenge of my quest and were instrumental in helping me put together a hunt schedule that made sense. But, they were also quick to remind me that exceptional bucks, especially record-book bucks, aren't found behind every tree, no matter how good the hunting area. No honest outfitter ever guarantees a big buck, especially hunting under strictly "fair-chase" conditions. In my estimation, I would be hunting with the best outfitters for each species and with guides who were known for consistently finding big bucks for their hunters.

After a little research, it became obvious that some of the species would require more than one hunt. My hunting schedule meant that over a period of six months I would be away from home for over 90 days. The grueling schedule generated little sympathy from my hunting friends. Luckily, I am blessed with a wife who understands my love of hunting, especially for deer, and she encouraged me to chase my dream.

My extensive preparation included a work-out schedule. Being in good physical condition would be critical to success. Even with the daily work-outs and the mountain of pre-hunt logistics to work through, time crept by until August and my first hunt.

I traveled the full length of North America and experienced some of the most beautiful country that any sportsman could hope to hunt. Along the way, I spent time with some of the finest people on earth— guides and outfitters who I consider friends. I will be eternally grateful for their contributions in my accomplishing what I believe was the first time all six major deer species were killed in one year.

At the end of my Deer Quest, the total gross score of my six best bucks was 828-2/8 points. The total for the B&C Awards level minimums was 845 points. Obviously, not all of the bucks beat my lofty goals, but these hunts gave me a new appreciation of what it takes to kill bucks that make the record book! On several hunts, because I wouldn't give up looking for that monster buck until the last few minutes of the hunt, I ended up shooting bucks that were smaller than others I had already passed up. It was a testament to my guides who stood with me when I passed up magnificent bucks that most clients would have been happy to kill. At the final count, I was able to tag eight bucks that I believe most people would agree were above average and, certainly, representative of their species.

I am getting to the age where hunting doesn't come as easily as it once did. In truth, the mountains seem steeper, the cold weather penetrates more, and the days are longer—especially when I spend day after day, and week after week, in the field. As the proverbial winter in my hunting career draws nearer, I am happy that I took a comparatively few days out of my remaining time and spent them deer hunting. The hunts of my Deer Quest generated good memories that will last the rest of my life. I hope the stories will entertain you and inform you, and perhaps my adventures will stir another deer hunter to take up the challenge of killing a "triple-double" in one year. For me, it was the Deer Quest of a lifetime. —LS

Blacktail
Deer

North America's Toughest Deer Trophy

T WO SPECIES of black-tailed deer, Columbia and Sitka, are now accepted by most recognized record book committees. The Sitka blacktail was not recognized as a separate species by Boone and Crockett record keepers until 1984, and a nontypical classification was only established recently.

Reliable blacktail trophy information and research has been accumulated by the Boone and Crockett Club (B&C), Safari Club International (SCI), and Pope and Young (P&Y) through developing antler-measuring systems, training certified measurers, reviewing entries, and producing the various record books. Published information from these record-keeping groups is invaluable in helping hunters decide where to hunt and establishing reasonable expectations. For example, if I wanted to kill a record-book Columbia blacktail, I would not choose to hunt in British Columbia because the data reveals that few record-size bucks are submitted from that province; thus, the prospect of killing a top-10 candidate is remote.

Blacktail Ranges

I have not had extensive experience hunting the Sitka blacktail, but I have killed dozens of the Columbia variety and believe that the current measuring systems reasonably separate the two species. I will provide here only a general description of the blacktail ranges. Of the two, the Columbia blacktail's range is the most extensive. They live in coastal areas from the edge of Monterey Bay, California, north through western California, Oregon, Washington, and British Columbia, including Vancouver Island.

Sitka blacktails are confined to southern Alaska, including Kodiak Island and surrounding islands, through southeastern Alaska into northern British Columbia. The southern boundary is Bella Coola, British Columbia, and includes the Queen Charlotte Islands nearly 35 miles offshore.

The boundaries for the mule deer and blacktails are difficult to describe because of interbreeding between the species wherever their ranges intersect. Therefore, no system of record keeping and description of these species will ever be perfect. All along the Columbia blacktail range there is a gray area where blacktails hybridize with mule deer. In my home state, Oregon, for example, interbreeding occurs along the west side of the Cascade Range. These blacktail-mule deer crosses are called locally "bench legs." These bucks are not likely to challenge the mule deer rankings, but they present a definite complication, if not a threat, to black-tail record listings.

I have personally refused to measure racks as blacktail entries because I believed that they were muley hybrids. That is one reason why the recent rules for photos of the tail and metatarsal gland on Columbia blacktails have become important. The mule deer's tail is a distinct rope-thin, black-tipped appendage. The wide tail of a blacktail, on the other hand, is shaped much like its cousin the whitetail, except it is shorter and narrower and has a broad strip of black hair running its length. A blacktail's metatarsal gland will measure 2-1/2 to 3 inches long and is located halfway between the hock and hoof. On the other hand, a muley's gland will measure at least 5 inches long and is positioned closer to the hock.

The Hunting Challenge

Probably no subject will get me into trouble faster than declaring one deer species more difficult to hunt and kill than the others. All hunters will have their own candidate for this title, opinions that I find usually favor the species that they have hunted the longest. Most experienced hunters, however, will agree that all North American deer offer a worthwhile hunting challenge, especially if you restrict yourself to hunting for big bucks. Sure, in some states it's legal to kill five deer a day, but you're not likely to kill five mature bucks.

I have been fortunate that for more than four decades I have hunted the various subspecies of deer across most of their ranges. Some years I tagged up to eight bucks, and even in the bad years I killed at least two. There have been countless hunts, though, where I couldn't find a good buck or where one just gave me the slip. There are hunters with more experience, but I feel that my 40-plus years of multi-species hunting have provided me with insight into the differences and difficulties of hunting the various deer and, I think, a basis to offer my opinion; in the end, that's all it is.

That said, I'm going ahead and climbing out on a limb to declare that if you're trying to kill a high-scoring buck, the Columbia blacktail is the most difficult species to hunt. My opinion is based on several factors. First, over most of their range, their preferred habitat creates some of the worst hunting conditions imaginable. The hills are frequently steep enough to challenge a sheep hunter and almost always are covered with thick foliage of thorny vines and soaking wet foliage. The high canopy of timber and brush can create a cathedral-like atmosphere accented by eerie dancing rays of filtered sunlight. The sprays of alternating shadow and light are beautiful, but make it a real challenge to spot a standing buck. It's common to plunge down a deer trail and suddenly find yourself flailing through a jungle of blackberries, scrub alders, tangled brush, rhododendrons, vines, and tropically lush ferns. Brush often reaches higher that your head, blotting out all landmarks. Visibility is also often limited to less than a few feet. Even when you can find a spot with reasonable visibility, the intertwined branches and thick, noisy brush make life miserable for hunters who covet quiet stalks. Blacktail hunts can turn into survival affairs where a hunter is elated to just bulldoze through the tangled growth and come out alive and reasonably unscratched. To make it worse, it's not unusual for blacktail bucks to simply freeze in the brush while hunters thrash past just a few feet away. The dense, almost tropical, habitat is one reason why many hunters target blacktails only once.

It's also why a lot of blacktail hunters drive logging roads, glassing for feeding and bedded deer in brushy clearcuts left from logging projects. Even this style of hunting is difficult because the brown-gray coat of a blacktail blends exceptionally well into their surroundings, and they can be tough to spot unless they move. Other hunters favor the waiting game and settle into stands at trail crossings, forest edges, clearcuts, and feeding areas. Most of the time, and almost always when the day is warm and dry, it's a better idea to let the deer come to the hunter than for the hunter to try to go to the deer.

Second, you have to contend with weather that's often punctuated by fog and bone-chilling, misty days. Even the most seasoned blacktail hunters admit that hunting under these conditions is just plain "no fun." When it's not raining, the ground is still muddy and the undergrowth is soaked because everything—moss, lichens, and leaves—soaks up the ample moisture. It's what causes many of us who hunt this country to throw away the Gore-Tex and put on the wools—you're going to get wet, so you might as well be warm.

Third, most blacktail hunting takes place on public property or vast tracts of land controlled by large timber companies. Some of the best Columbia blacktail areas are within an hour or two driving time from state and provincial population centers, and hunting pressure can be heavy. It makes the big bucks very wary. Even during the off-hunting season these areas are popular with recreationalists, including hikers, mushroom gatherers, mountain bikers, motorcyclists, horse riders, fern pickers, campers, and sightseers. This activity is compounded by loggers who frequent the forest year around. These pressures condition many bucks, especially older ones, to become nocturnal. Biologists did a study several years ago in the southern part of Oregon, proving that most movement, especially by older, bigger bucks, occurred long before sunup. Pictures of trophy bucks collected using motion-triggered cameras were mind-boggling. It was intimidating for those of us who have hunted this country to see the number and quality of bucks evading us.

Finally, a blacktail is still, in the eyes of many hunters, a runt mule deer. That's simply not true! Renowned wildlife biologist, Dr. Valerius Geist, has proved through DNA analyses that the mule deer actually descended from crossbreeding between the whitetail and blacktail. Regrettably, for trophy hunters, blacktails didn't retain the "big-rack" gene, possibly an evolutionary concession to its jungle-like habitat. Most good blacktail racks are beautiful, however. The tines are stout, often burnished a striking cedar color, and form an attractive basket shape. I also believe that a blacktail's cape, with its dark ochre coloration and black chevron, makes the most striking mount in the deer family. Unfortunately, the rack of a giant blacktail would cradle well inside even a mediocre mule deer, which is another reason why it "gets no respect" from many hunters.

These are the reasons why I believe that the Columbia blacktail is the most underhunted and underrated deer in North America. I admit, though, that if for some reason I could only hunt one deer species, blacktail would not be my first choice. Still, the difficulty of killing a truly big blacktail buck can't be overstated. It's a special challenge to go one-on-one against a wise old buck on its own tangled turf.

Many of these same points also apply to Sitka blacktails, which live in equally tough country where hunting is often under miserable conditions. Sitka blacktails are found in absolutely wild remote island areas almost devoid of hunting pressure, and hunting for them is a remarkable experience, but certainly of a lesser challenge than hunting their southern cousins. In addition, many of the best bucks are killed in November, when high-country snows and the rut bring them down to the beaches at the edge of saltwater where hunters can reach them with boats. For these reasons, my nod goes to the Columbia blacktail.

For almost three decades I have lived in some of the best Columbia blacktail country in North America and have hunted them hard. I've taken a few good bucks, but I've had many more great bucks elude me. One that stands out in my mind is a buck that I tried to pin down for two years. Many hunters saw him from time to time, but he always disappeared before hunting season. A popular story was that he was finally killed by a car at night and was buried by the farmer on whose land he stayed most of the time. I suspect, though, that he was poached, because everyone would get strangely vague when I offered to dig up the 5 x 5 buck with a reported spread of 28 inches—certainly, a top-ranking contender. Another big buck I hunted for several years stayed on private ground owned by a strict anti-hunter, and I could never ambush him on the adjoining farm.

My best typical buck, scored 156-5/8 SCI points and ranked as number two in the SCI records for a time, was taken in southern Oregon. Killing that buck was largely because of my good friend, Perry Allen. He spotted the buck during one of his many pre-season scouting trips and called me late one summer evening to tell me that he found a world record contender. Imagine a friend willing to share a buck like that! Perry kept track of the buck throughout the summer, always at a safe distance and never penetrating into his home turf. He watched him from a long distance through binoculars and checked his movements by searching the surrounding trails for tracks. Perry told me that we needed to be hunting a specific slope on opening day.

Long before daylight I was climbing steep, unfamiliar slopes and plowing through brush thickets on my way to a spot marked on my map. I'd never been there, but I had confidence that Perry knew best. However, after about a half hour of cussing and brush busting, I'll admit that I had my doubts about the sanity of the plan.

At dawn, though, I was recovering from my death march, while sitting several hundred yards away from two clearcuts on the facing slope. Ribbons of trees and brush divided the clearcuts and provided perfect bedding areas for the buck and several other deer Perry had seen earlier. Over the next hour, I watched a few deer feeding there, but there was no sign of the big buck. Perry was still hunting his way across the slopes, and occasionally I would catch a glimpse of him moving through the thick cover. When he reached the last stand of trees, he motioned me over to him. It was my turn to fight the brush again.

Working my way down the slope, I had just crossed a creek when a truckload of hunters pulled up on a log landing several hundred yards above me. The hunters climbed out and glassed the clearcut that I was just entering. There's no sense playing dog for someone else, so I waited and watched for several minutes until they climbed into their pickup and charged off down the road. Apparently, they didn't see me. For sure they didn't see the big buck or the other deer that exploded out from almost under my feet when I moved. One shot and it was over!

The only thing that remained was to pay the price for hunting in such a hellhole. Packing him straight up to the landing, even though it was fewer than 500 yards above us, was out of the question. The slope was so steep we could hardly stand. It took hours for the two of us to tug, pull, jerk, and drag the buck across the thick brush in the clearcuts to Perry's pickup parked on a logging road. Such is the penalty many of us endure when hunting blacktails. On this hunt, though, we at least had something to show for our pain and suffering.

Quality Trophies

I know that it's an overused statement, but the quality of the trophy really is in the eye of the beholder. Certainly, the measure of a hunt isn't simply who can kill the most bucks. For many of us the quality of the hunting experience is the most important part of hunting. For me, though, it adds so much more to the hunting experience when I collect an outstanding representative of the species. I've killed more than 150 bucks during my hunting career, and I'm long past the need to kill deer just to prove that I can. I don't want to kill a buck if it means killing a small buck. This discipline is one of the ways that I maximize the challenge of my hunts and thereby add to the hunting experience. I know that I pass up deer every year that would give many hunters the shakes.

Part of the reason I wrote this book is to put hunters on the right track to locating big blacktails. Without any doubt, the best Sitka blacktails have been taken on Alaska's Kodiak Island and its neighboring Alaskan islands. There are also some fine trophies on the islands off southeast Alaska, and Prince of Wales Island has some of the biggest.

Hot spots for trophy Columbia blacktails are scattered across three states. California lays claim to the most record book entries, Oregon earns the second most, and Washington is a distant third. However, if you're after the largest bucks, Oregon is the place to hunt. Of the top ten B&C entries, Washington has three entries, including the world record, Oregon has six, and California the remaining listing. In southern Oregon, hunters should look in Douglas and Jackson Counties, and in northern Oregon, they should concentrate on Marion and Clackamas Counties. In Washington, the top areas are largely rural Cowlitz and Lewis Counties in the southwest part of the state. In California, Trinity County has produced not only many bucks, but big ones as well. The Yolla Bolly Wilderness is a good bet for big bucks, but hunters should be in excellent physical condition before tackling this steep, roadless region.

Mossyhorns
Of
Trinity County

I**T MUST HAVE BEEN** a trophy hunter who coined the saying, "Sometimes it's better to be lucky than good!" Lady Luck has probably helped me on several of my most memorable hunts. I'm dead certain she was crouched in the rocks beside me on that incredible mid-August morning in the coastal mountains of northern California.

Everything about that late summer hunt was special. I was hunting specifically for a big Columbia blacktail buck, and I was hunting with Jim and TinaMarie Schaafsma, owners of Arrow Five Outfitters, who have built their well-deserved reputation by producing monster blacktails.

Light was just easing into the sky on the first day of blacktail hunting season when Jim, his guide trainee Brandon Trone, and I left camp. When we started down into the canyon, the warm fingers of sunlight were poking into the thickets of manzanita brush just enough for us to distinguish antler tines from twisted branches. Our descent into the deep canyon below the house was fairly typical. We had seen at least a dozen deer, including several respectable bucks, by the time we cleared the last gate. None of the bucks, however, drew more than a second glance. We were looking for something special. Little did I know how special the day was going to be!

TinaMarie, Jim's wife and a very capable guide in her own right, was with three other hunters, Mitch and Cody Besso and Greg White, who were hunting wild pigs and a management buck. As we cleared the crest of a small rise, we saw their pickup silhouetted against the skyline on a knob only a short distance away. All four were intently glassing a meadow at the base of the ridge. Quietly, we eased over to their vantage point and focused our binoculars on the shadows and trees surrounding the meadow.

TinaMarie quickly pointed out a buck that Greg had spotted in the meadow. Then she said the magic word, "nontypical," and my interest spiked. Big, nontypical blacktails are very rare. In fact, B&C didn't even have a category for a nontypical Columbia blacktail until recently. Luckily for me, none of TinaMarie's hunters had booked a trophy hunt.

Two smaller bucks, which had been feeding with the big buck, had already left the open meadow and disappeared into the oak groves, probably headed toward a midday bedding area where getting a clean shot would be tough. And the one we were watching was almost ready to join them. I'm sure that it was Lady Luck who enticed the buck to continue feeding instead of following his buddies into that dense bedding area where visibility would be limited.

Through my spotting scope it was immediately obvious that this buck wasn't just any old nontypical buck, sporting a few sticker points. Instead, I could see clearly an extra main beam and two eye guards. Jim sweetened the pot when he said, "He's got double eye guards on both sides."

I hesitated because I was having trouble estimating his gross score. As if he read my mind, Jim offered, "I think he'll score in the 140s." That, and the fact that I was looking at the only nontypical blacktail I had ever seen, brought me to my senses. After a short discussion, we bent as low to the ground as humanly possible and slipped down the open slope toward a rocky outcropping. Halfway there, I sneaked a peek and was surprised to see the buck looking our way. Imagine what was going through my mind! But once again, Lady Luck smiled. The buck dropped his head and continued feeding. Finally, we arrived at the rocks, where a tree gave us some cover. Quickly, I slid out into prone position alongside its trunk.

Cranking my Leupold up and the bipod down, I was ready. "How far?" I asked. Jim estimated the shot at a little over 300 yards, and I agreed. At that range it was point blank for my 7mm

The author has good reason to smile while holding his first-day trophy. Its third main beam makes it a truly exceptional trophy, although any nontypical Columbia blacktail is rare.

magnum shooting a 150-grain bullet. All I had to do was execute the shot. When I looked back into the scope, the buck was facing directly away. The velvet-covered massive antlers looked impressive. After what seemed like an eternity, he took a step to his left, giving me a quartering-away shot. I figured I could slip one past his hip and up into the boiler room.

"Ready?" I whispered.

"Go," he replied, as I squeezed the trigger.

As the recoil kicked the barrel up, I caught a glimpse of the buck racing for the trees. "You hit him!" Jim shouted. "I could see blood as he ran. We'll find him down there." I hoped so. I had made a rookie mistake and hadn't marked where the buck disappeared into the trees.

True to Jim's word, we walked straight to the buck crumpled just inside the tree line. As I approached him, my only thought was, "God, look at that mass!" There was definitely no ground shrinkage on this one! He did, indeed, have double eye guards on both sides, with a 4 x 3 main frame and a third main beam that seemingly went on forever. I just stared at my monstrous 5 x 7 blacktail, a true one-in-a-million trophy, and quietly thanked Lady Luck for being in my corner—again.

As we were preparing to go back to camp, Jim and I couldn't resist trying to guess his score. I came up with 152 points, while Jim estimated 148 points. Official measurements later confirmed that the buck had a gross score of 147-7/8 points. Don't you hate it when your guide shows off? With a total mass measurement of over 36 inches and a third main beam length of 15-5/8 inches, combined with the double eye guards, he was everything I could have possibly hoped to find.

I have the buck mounted in my trophy room on an eye-catching pedestal; he still has the antler velvet on. Besides being in perfect shape, the velvet has unusual silver streaks radiating up the main beams. After the 60-day waiting period, the buck qualified as the new number eight nontypical Columbia Blacktail in the SCI record book.

I was disappointed that my hunt was over, but it allowed us several days to scout before the next hunter, Gary Sorensen, arrived. It also gave me a chance to help two youngsters on their hunts, and I enjoyed going along with these eager young deerstalkers almost as much as my own hunt. It was especially satisfying to watch 12-year-old Cody Mallo kill his first deer and Cody Besso anchor the largest buck of his young hunting career.

The Next Generation's Hunts

That afternoon, after we skinned my buck and put the meat in the cooler, Jim and I joined Mitch and Cody Besso on the hunt for Cody's buck. For a change of pace, we headed up a road that parallels the east boundary of the ranch and leads into prime hunting country where I had spotted big bucks several years earlier.

Partway up the mountain, we hiked out to "TinaMarie's Rock," an overlook with a sweeping view that has been her favorite lookout for years. We settled in behind our glasses, and it wasn't long before we started spotting deer. The bucks were still

An amply supply of acorns is one reason why big Columbia blacktail thrive in California.

herded in bachelor groups and were feeding in open meadows, giving us an advantage. In several weeks, acorns, a favorite food for blacktails, would start dropping, and the deer would be drawn back into the dense groves of white and black oaks.

As we sat there, it became almost monotonous, with each of us whispering the magic words, "There's a buck," or even better, "There's a couple!" We were experiencing a common problem on this ranch; the bucks were either too big or too small for Cody's management buck. Jim was committed to trying to find Cody a respectable buck, but we kept kidding the youngster that we were looking for the smallest two-point buck on the ranch.

Despite the dozens of deer we could see from TinaMarie's Rock, we couldn't turn any of them into a shootable buck and continued working up the mountain. Just short of the top, we came to a long grass meadow, flanked by trees disappearing into a gully. As we approached the only gully crossing, Mitch yelled, "Stop!" and pointed to a group of five nervous bucks milling in the bottom. Suddenly, one bolted into the trees. I raised my glasses. The first several bucks I saw were too big, and then I found one that was "just right!" The 2 x 3 buck was wide and appeared to be older—a perfect candidate because he would probably never get bigger. When I heard Mitch say, "That one's a shooter!" I glued my attention on the deer.

At the shot the buck seemed to slump before running into the gully and up the far bank where another buck was standing. At the second shot, I was stunned to see the bigger buck fall "deader than a mackerel." I looked around with my mouth wide open. "He shot the wrong one!" I gasped. The joke was on me, though, because

Mitch had upgraded Cody's hunt so that he could take a better buck, only I didn't know it. You have to love a dad like that!

Jim and Mitch both assured me that Cody had hit the same buck twice, and when we got down to him, two entrance holes proved them right. The 2 x 3 buck I was watching must have slipped when it was startled by the first shot. Any avid blacktail hunter would appreciate Cody's buck. Back at camp, the 5 x 6 rack would gross 128-6/8 points.

More importantly, its mount will serve as a lasting reminder for this 17 year old of a special time with his father.

It was also a special day for me, since we had taken two great bucks. The impressive quality of bucks produced by Arrow Five Outfitters is one of the reasons that I was hunting with the Schaafsmas on my Deer Quest. On my first hunt with them, I saw many bucks, including two outstanding trophies. Despite our best efforts, both of the monster blacktails got away, but the images of those two giant bucks were burned into my memory. That's why when I began putting together my Deer Quest, one of my first calls was to Jim and TinaMarie. I could think of nowhere in North America where a hunter would have a better chance to tag a trophy blacktail.

Jim has hunted the nearly 12,000-acre Stewart Ranch east of Eureka, California, for a dozen years. When he started, surveys indicated a fawn survival rate under 30 percent. Jim implemented several conservation programs, including strict predator controls, and after several years of hunting the ranch on his own, he enrolled the ranch in California's Private Land Management (PLM) program. Under this program, landowners are issued a limited number of hunting permits in exchange for implementing a state-approved wildlife management plan. As an incentive, landowners are allowed to set ranch hunting seasons within state guidelines. Don't for a second think that the plan is just a formality. The PLM program is proving to be an exceptional wildlife program, but it requires a large investment in money, effort, and time—all dedicated to wildlife.

Deer aren't the only wildlife benefiting from the PLM program. On the Stewart ranch, the program also includes work done for wood ducks, quail, and the pigs, not to mention a study on the oak's acorn production. It's a comprehensive plan that includes water and range improvements that far exceed public lands' enhancement programs. Years later, the numbers prove the value of this management approach. For example, ranch deer counts now peg fawn survival at 75 percent, an increase of 45 percent. More than 700 blacktails roam the ranch, and the buck/doe ratio is more than 65 bucks per 100 does.

Within the PLM program, Arrow Five Outfitters and the ranch owners, the Stewarts, have found that carefully designed hunt plans and balanced harvest ratios are critical to long-term herd success and maximum trophy production. Jim allows only 10 trophy buck hunts a year and 20 management hunts, which include five donated youth hunts. They also take only a maximum of 15 does. That's the total annual deer harvest—hardly a dent in the population. It's a big reason why Arrow Five Outfitters accounts for many of the top entries in the record books. Obviously, this approach allows the big bucks to grow to their full potential. It's also a reason why I was there a second time!

That night, after we took care of Cody's buck, we were sitting around the campfire, and the conversation drifted to hunting stories past and present. Jim caught my attention when he began describing a buck he had watched a month earlier. The rack was still growing, he said, adding, "I think he's going to be a good one!" As I listened to Jim paint his word picture of that beautiful buck, I could almost see him through the dancing orange and red flames of the campfire.

Kevin Mallo and our next hunter, his son Cody, arrived that night. Each year, Jim and TinaMarie donate five hunts to the local hunters education programs. Every hunter who passes the program is eligible to win one of the ranch hunts for a management deer, and Cody was lucky to draw one! For many of the youths, it is their first chance venturing into the field carrying a rifle on a deer hunt, and in some cases, their first time hunting. That alone was worth the price of admission for me.

Our young hunter was excited and eager when we left camp early the next morning, looking for his management buck. Again, we found plenty of bucks. The problem was sorting out one that was better than "just a buck," but still with the age and rack development that qualified it for removal from the herd. Cody was shooting an open-sighted .30-.30, which limited his effective shooting range.

Cody Mallo is not enjoying the experience of gutting his first deer.

At midday, we had blown several attempts and spotted numerous "almost" bucks. We were driving down a remote ranch road toward camp when suddenly, a large-framed 5 x 6, buck streaked cross the road. It was far too big to shoot, but a second buck quietly lying in the cool grass off to the side would fit the management-buck bill nicely! Jim and Cody slipped out of the truck and crept forward. Cody levered in a round, took careful aim, and pulled the trigger.

Immediately, the buck was up and running, and just as fast, the hunters were in hot pursuit. Then, almost inexplicably, the buck made a fatal mistake and turned back. I supposed he was trying to follow his buddy that left him "holding the bag." One more shot and it was over. Cody had his buck, and he couldn't have been happier—except for one minor detail. As a part of the hunting experience, Jim expects his new hunters to clean their own buck. Of course, they get some help. Cody was a little reluctant at first. His first shot had nicked the paunch, so the gutting task was no picnic. Still, taking care of a downed animal is a part of hunting, and to Cody's credit, he finished the job.

We dropped the meat off at the camp cooler and, with a few hours of good daylight left, we headed to the west side of the ranch for an evening scouting trip. It was one of those glorious days—clear, warm, but not too hot, with white fluffy clouds that made you want to lie back on the grass and just dream. Instead, another hunter was to arrive in two days, and we still had to locate a good buck for him.

We were dropping into the valley again when Jim pointed toward a tree-choked gully not 200 yards away and said, "There's a good one!" Several deer were visible in the oaks, and one buck really stood out. He was noticeably heavier than the other four in the bunch and had the look of a real trophy. The buck definitely demanded closer inspection. They were working up the gully toward a seep at the base of a rock bluff. At one point, the buck climbed to the top of the far bank and presented us with a perfect skyline view. Rim light illuminated the velvet rack so beautifully that I was tempted to put down my binoculars and grab a camera.

Instead, I grabbed my spotting scope and cranked it up to 45x. Even under that high magnification, I couldn't see many point deductions on the rack. The G-3 appeared to be several inches short on one side, but it only appeared short because the other side was outstanding! After scratching our guesses in the dirt, we agreed that he would gross between 143 and 145 points, a fine trophy. Finding that buck was a capper to a typically great day on this ranch. Driving back to camp that night we agreed that we had seen 38 branch-antlered bucks. Locating the big boy took a little pressure off Jim, who likes to have one or two bucks spotted before his clients arrive.

The next morning we were up scouting again at the crack of dawn. A thin wafer of fog was slowly creeping up the valley and soon engulfed us as we dropped toward the valley floor. However, it was already beginning to burn off, salvaging the morning scouting trip.

We were headed toward the power house on the creek several thousand feet below camp. On the way we expected to find from 10 to 20 bucks feeding in the meadows and oak thickets that dotted the valley sides. We could only hope to find the big skyline buck again, or at least another buck that would score a minimum of 130 points.

It didn't take long to jump the first buck. When I swung open the second gate, a small 2 x 3 scampered up the mountain. For the next 45 minutes, we kept spotting deer; a couple of does here and a buck there. None, however, were what we were looking for, so we moved steadily. The sun had not yet cleared the east hills, and the creek bottom, still wrapped in shadow, was still cool. Jim figured that the bucks would continue to feed until the sun slipped above the ridge line and warmed the slopes.

I had just finished glassing the full length of a strip of trees and had started back again when I spotted four bucks low on a ridge where just minutes before there had been nothing. Apparently, the deer had just stepped out of the trees. I focused my binoculars, and suddenly there he was! It wasn't the skyline buck, but it was a dandy. Jim quickly located the buck and we started trading comments on his rack. We really tried, but couldn't grow a fourth tine on his right beam. Still, he would obviously gross over 130 points. Jim finally said, "He isn't the one we're trying to find." Imagine hunting where you can look nonchalantly at a buck that would be a contender for B&C recognition. And two out of the other three bucks traveling with him were no slouches! It took real determination to turn my glasses away from those bucks.

The thin fog line was starting to burn off from the top of the ridge, above where I was busy concentrating my search along its west end. The meadows were too far away for my binoculars, which I swapped for my spotting scope. As soon as I focused the scope on the hillside, I spotted a small buck. Less than 20 yards away from it there was an indistinct movement in the grass. I finally made out the form of a buck lying belly deep in the tall tan grass.

"Jim, there's a buck bedded on that far ridge, but I can't see his main beam," I said. It took me a moment to figure out that I was looking at an extremely heavy, high-forked buck. He simply dwarfed the 3 x 3 running with him.

Suddenly, Jim was very interested! It seems that Jim and several clients had tried to kill this buck for the last two seasons. Although he wouldn't be a book contender, he was an interesting blacktail. Jim told me that the buck spent most of his time deep in the safety of a long brushy draw that ran from the ridge line to the river thousands of feet below. It was no wonder that he grew old outwitting hunters. The massive fork horn was one of several bucks we saw that morning. We left early, grabbed some lunch at camp, and then drove to the airport where Gary Sorensen, Jim's next hunter, would be arriving.

One for the Book

Within minutes after Gary landed, we were bending his ear with stories about what we had found. Most of our stories centered on the huge 4 x 4 skyline buck. Surprisingly, Gary seemed unexcited. Then I learned that he had hunted with Jim before, had seen giant bucks, and already knew that a patient man could be rewarded with the "buck of a lifetime."

The next morning we were up before dawn and out at first light. Our plan was to cross to the other side of the valley and look back at the slope where we had watched the skyline buck. Jim, Gary, and I were on the move, climbing further up the ridge. Last night's fog moved along on a gentle wind, one minute creating pockets of filtered light and the next an impenetrable mask. It was raising havoc with our efforts; from time to time obscuring the buck's favorite hideout on the face of the far ridge. Finally, Jim said, "Let's go."

We had traveled less than a mile and just rounded a sharp corner when Gary said, "There!" He pointed down the ridge to where three bucks were slowly sifting through the trees. The bucks were cautious, but not spooked. The rack on the biggest buck was very heavy and wide, but his 3 x 3 tines were shorter than what Gary wanted. Still, he was a great buck, with mass and velvet that looked almost white, giving me the impression that he was long past his prime. Jim got out of the pickup to get a different glassing angle into the brush.

We watched the bucks for several minutes, hoping that a bigger buck was still hidden back in the oaks. It seemed that we were wasting our time. Gary wasn't going to shoot, and I wanted to get up the mountain.

Suddenly, Jim broke the silence with, "There they are!" I couldn't figure out where he was looking, and before I could ask, he slid in behind the wheel and we started moving. The skyline buck, he said, was on the opposite side of the valley. We didn't have to go far before finding a better vantage point. Jim and I slid behind our spotting scopes. Immediately, my lens filled with the magnificent buck that we had been trying to locate again for Gary.

The skyline buck looked just as good as the last time we watched him. As Jim and I excitedly chattered back and forth about the monster buck, Gary was strangely silent. From his past hunts here he knew that this ranch supported many outstanding bucks, and shooting on the first morning bothered him. At the same time, you can't look a gift horse in the mouth!

As we watched, the bucks fed across a small meadow and into an oak thicket. The bachelor group was headed toward the seep under the rocky bluff where we saw them the previous day. We folded up our scopes and hustled to a road cutting across the top of the ridge, just above the bluff. As we walked down the slope, Gary announced, "I'm going to wait until at least 9 o'clock to shoot!" Jim and I chuckled. We kept walking until we reached the rock knob where we hoped to catch the bucks crossing below us.

Jim was the first to spot the bucks coming up the gully, and he and Gary scrambled to get into shooting position beside a tree. I sat farther back and waited. And waited. It seemed that Gary was taking forever to get squared away for the shot; first he tried

A blacktail lying in a clearcut can be very difficult to spot and stalk. The country behind this clearcut shows the wide variety of cover where a blacktail can stay hidden from hunters.

kneeling, then sitting, then standing, then leaning over a branch. He even tried bracing on shooting sticks that Jim had retrieved from his pack. I was getting nervous. Gary looked back at me and pointed to his wrist, sans a wristwatch. I glanced down at my watch. Three minutes before nine. Close enough! I signaled, okay.

I jumped at the crack of the .257 Weatherby, but definitely heard the "whomp" of the bullet hitting home. His first shot was followed by an insurance shot, and the skyline buck was his. While we were scrambling off the knob, I couldn't help but kid Gary about waiting to shoot until the buck grew larger. "No," he said. "I told you I didn't want to shoot until 9 o'clock!" Now, that's what I call confidence!

The velvet-encased 4 x 4 rack scored 140-5/8 points, which was admittedly less than we thought, but still it was a great blacktail buck. The smallest tine was nearly 6 inches long, and the buck had great eye guards. Mass measurements of nearly 16 inches to a side were only accentuated by the velvet, which was in perfect condition. It was an exceptionally attractive trophy and will make a striking mount.

Finding and watching Gary drop the skyline buck was a fitting conclusion to one of my great hunts. I had been involved with the harvesting of three exceptional trophies and a management buck that brought a great deal of joy to a new hunter. In four days, I was treated to the thrill of watching over 100 bucks, including at least a dozen that would qualify as blacktail trophies under anybody's evaluation. I wouldn't have expected anything less from Arrow Five Outfitters.

Blacktail
in the Land
of the
Midnight Sun

M Y FRIENDS, Don Causey, Wayne Long, and I walked only a
short distance up the shallow creek before we came to pools
and riffles literally choked with Coho salmon. We were
following a narrow path and keeping a watchful eye out for any
dark shape in the shadows whenever the path detoured back into the
trees. Alaska brownies were enjoying their fall ritual of splurging on
the ample spawning salmon, and none of us wanted to push our
luck. Stories of harrowing encounters between fishermen and
opportunistic bears looking for an easy meal fired our imagination.

The trail was littered with tattered salmon parts and many fresh
carcasses. Evidence of giant bears was even more ominous when
we entered a long meadow, not far from a small lake that was the
creek's source. Worn trails crisscrossed through waist-high sedge
grass lining the creek, punctuated by matted areas the size of a car
that were strewn with fish parts. I was lugging a camera case
because I wanted to take some action photos of Don catching
acrobatic Cohos. Don is the owner and publisher of the Hunting
and Angling Reports, so I was looking forward to some fishing
tips. For insurance I also carried my .300 Remington Ultra Mag
fed with 200-grain Barnes bullets—certainly potent bear medicine,
if it came to that. It gave us a sense of well-being and safety!

Our wilderness bliss was shattered, however, when we returned
to our boat anchored in the inlet. Skipper Brian Kewan yelled the
terrible news. "A plane has hit the World Trade Center!" That
announcement hit us like a brick. We had intended to fish for a
while longer, but after a quick conference, we turned the bow of

the boat into the wind and headed for Kodiak. Along the way, we were glued to the radio, like millions of other Americans, getting one terrible update after another. By the time we arrived at the dock, the horrible events of that day were well documented.

As we swung the bag with the cape and horns of my coveted Sitka blacktail onto the dock, I remember thinking how trivial our adventure was in comparison to the horrors faced by the victims' families. Even though we were thousands of miles away, the long tentacles of terrorism had reached out and affected our lives in ways that we would never forget. It certainly put perspective on the value of life and the importance of living every minute to its fullest!

Recognition of our mortality is one of the many of reasons why I hunt. It gives my life balance—enjoyment and the wonderment of watching wildlife and nature. Only a few days earlier I had been sitting on the deck of our lodge with a hot cup of coffee, watching the dawn break and warm the tops of the mountains across from the lodge. Crimson fields of fireweed dotting the lower slopes were just beginning to show at their best. The mountain's reflection was mirrored in the glass-smooth fiord, broken only by the anchored boats raised to dock level by high tide. Overhead, two eagles screeched to each other as they flew from their nest in the towering trees surrounding the lodge, heading out to gorge on salmon left by the bears that night. Life was good!

Through my spotting scope, set on the deck railing, I could watch blacktail deer feeding on the opposite mountainside. I was at the remote lodge on a self-guided hunt for Sitka blacktail and the second leg of my Deer Quest.

Fortunately, I had been invited to join Wayne, his wife Sherry, and Don on this exploratory trip to Afognak Island. Wayne is the President of Multiple Use Managers Alaska (MUM) and had been in discussions with the Afognak Native Corporation (ANC) for months. They were exploring the benefits of several revolutionary wildlife management projects.

MUM is plowing unbroken ground in Alaska. The Alaska Native Claims Settlement Act, passed in the early 1970s, ceded about 44 million acres to Alaskan natives, settling aboriginal land claims and clearing the way for construction of the trans-Alaska oil pipeline. Twelve native Alaskan corporations now control this huge chunk of land, and they are facing a myriad of problems, including a decline of subsistence hunting. Several areas have recently been restricted to subsistence hunting only, creating conflicts between natives and non-native hunters.

A look at moose population numbers provides a glimpse into the magnitude of the problem. Alaska supports approximately 155,000 moose in an area several times larger than Norway, Sweden, and Finland combined. Yet, those three Scandinavian countries have 10 times as many moose and annually harvest over 200,000 animals!

Why is Alaska's problem important to the rest of us? Well, don't think for a second that our right to hunt on public land will supercede the subsistence rights of natives. We made that mistake 20 years ago here in the Northwest with our fishing rights. I hope that we learned our lesson and can prevent permanently losing hunting rights on the huge tract of land at stake in Alaska. In fact, much of the 44 million acres of ceded native land is closed to non-native hunting today. MUM's discussion with the various native corporations offers some hope that sound wildlife management projects can be introduced in time to allow hunting in the future.

The value of private land wildlife management has been proven in the lower 48 states. Some of the strengths of Private Lands Management (PLM) projects include resource census and big game herd composition studies and habitat improvements, among other activities aimed at enhancement and treatment of wildlife as a carefully managed resource. Well-managed properties have shown dramatic increases not only in the quantity, but also the trophy quality of the big game. PLM projects are dramatic evidence that wildlife managers, landowners, and the outfitting industry can work together!

Most of the best deer and elk hunting in the West today occurs on privately managed lands, such as Santa Rosa Island, the Cooperative

Wildlife Management lands in Utah, or a number of native reservations, including the White Mountain, Mescalero, and Jicarilla lands, to name only a few.

Many Alaskan native corporations already have viable timber, mining, and fishing industries, so it is only a short step to maximize yet another of their many resources—wildlife. Drawing on its long history of producing results for other landowners, MUM is on the leading edge in helping native corporations to achieve the maximum benefits for wildlife. The payoff will be improved game populations for natives and hunters and improved business opportunities for guides and outfitters. If the native corporations obtain the same results as PLM management in the lower 48 states, the results will also mean larger trophies.

I was hunting Afognak in September because I wanted a "real hunt" for Sitka blacktail. My hunt would entail a steep climb from the lodge every day. Deer at this time of the year are found in the high country, often at the top of the highest mountains in the area. If I had waited until late October or November, I would have had two advantages. By late fall, the rut is raging, but the biggest advantage to this time of year is that the bucks would be lower on the hillsides, sometimes right on the beach. I've hunted under both conditions and prefer the challenge of an early mountaintop hunt.

Earlier in Kodiak, Peter Olsen, ANC land manager and my host, met me at the local Best Western. Although Peter couldn't join us at the lodge, he put us in the capable hands of Frank and Jean McLucas. Brian (in addition to running the boat) and Frank were in charge of security for ANC. Jean is the master of the lodge and one of the best cooks I've ever enjoyed on a hunt. Before Peter gave us a ride to the dock located on the other side of the island, I bought three deer tags and completed the licensing paperwork in Kodiak.

Not too many people are aware that the ANC offers a land use permit system allowing non-natives access to over 160,000 acres of prime hunting country. ANC controls land on Afognak, Raspberry, and Kodiak Islands. Non-native use and activities are limited to specific permit areas and zones, with local restrictions. For example, in some areas only foot traffic is allowed, and in others there are camping restrictions. A word of warning; these are real wilderness experiences and not for the faint of heart or body. Hunters who can't walk or climb while carrying a pack stuffed with meat will be better off booking a boat hunt and cruising the shoreline later in the season.

A $125 annual fee allows hunting on ANC lands and includes a deer endorsement (permit). In most areas, the bag limit is set by the Alaska Department of Fish and Game (ADFG). Generally, the annual limit is three or more deer. However, in one ANC area on Kodiak Island the limit is one. Permits are also available for hunting brown bear (guide required) or Roosevelt elk. In addition to ANC fees, state licenses and permits are also required. The land use permit issued by the ANC is not a hunting or fishing license, and in some cases limited big game permits are allocated by ADFG drawing. I suggest that you thoroughly read the ADFG regulations before contacting the ANC well in advance of an anticipated hunt. I had plenty of help with the proper paperwork from Peter and Wayne.

Our two-hour boat ride to the lodge that first day was too short because after we crossed Raspberry Strait between Kodiak and Afognak Islands, every turn revealed another beautiful panorama. Seals and sea otters played on the ocean's surface, while a variety of sea birds and gulls circled overhead. I could smell the salt air, and the fresh spray from the small swells slapping the boat confirmed that we were, indeed, moving farther and farther from civilization. The lodge is tucked in the back of Muskomee Bay, where it is protected from the worst of the howling winds and storms common to this area of Alaska.

We arrived at the beautiful, two-story log lodge late in the day, and it only took a few minutes to haul our bags up the boardwalk to our rooms. After enjoying a meal fit for a king, augmented with seafood fresh from the ocean, we made plans for the next morning. Frank suggested that we walk from the lodge to the tops of the surrounding mountains. That meant a climb of several thousand feet from sea level. On a topographical map, he pointed out one mountain to the south where he had seen bucks only a few days earlier. Frank was busy the next day, but Brian would be able to go. Wayne and Don came with us to see more of the island and maybe spot some of the Roosevelt elk that inhabit the area.

We left the lodge at dawn under the pall of a forecasted storm. In this country, a storm normally means rain, wind, mountain-shrouding clouds, and misery. We decided that the best approach would be to drop down to the creek feeding the bay, swing east around the mountain, and slowly gain elevation. At first, it was easy going along a well-worn trail through the forest. Then we found something lying in the trail that made our hair stand on end: the grisly remains of several partially eaten salmon that were still wet! It didn't take much convincing to get us off the trail and heading up a ridgeback. We weren't trying very hard to be quiet, either.

When the ridge petered out, we blazed our own path through the brush. It was bothering me that there weren't any game trails. It soon became painfully obvious why many hunters prefer to hunt at sea level in November. As we climbed, we would occasionally see what appeared to be grass-covered meadows offering decent walking conditions, but the grass only hid a matrix of channels and eroded cuts choked with downed trees and brush. It didn't take long to change our minds about walking there. On the positive side, the forecasted storm held off, and we weren't plagued by the notorious swarms of biting gnats and mosquitoes that make life unbearable in the summer.

It looked like our easiest route to the top would be to climb the ridge across from the mountain we eventually wanted to hunt. While we were climbing, visibility was restricted, but it didn't make any difference since it was impossible to walk quietly in the brush. At times, we just put our heads down and bulled ahead. It was so thick that we had to take turns leading. The stunted spruce thickets were the worst—too short to walk under and almost too thick to plow through. Then there were the alders! It was pure hell!

Although the temperature was crisp when we left the lodge, we soon shucked off our coats. It was a questionable trade-off between comfort and remaining unscathed. If we wore coats, we suffered from the heat, and if we took them off, we lost what little protection we had from the clutching branches and needlelike thorns of Devils club—a broad-leafed, spiny plant put on this earth to torture hunters. During one of our frequent short breaks, I glanced down at my watch and discovered that it had been pulled off my wrist as I plowed through the brush. I asked Don for the time and was shocked to learn that we had been climbing for over five hours. I took consolation in the fact that we were almost on top.

Eventually, the tangled thicket of alders and spruce gave way to scattered brush and low-growing ground cover. We stopped at the base of a basin leading toward a low pass and sat down to glass the surrounding hills. It didn't take two minutes for Wayne to whisper, "There's some," as he pointed to the top of the ridge to our left.

I soon saw three does climbing in the rocks, apparently on their way to bed down. We had to hurry. It was already getting late, and I was worried that the bucks may have already bedded down for the day in the impassible thickets. Swinging my glasses south to the pass, I picked up a deer on the skyline. Fog partially obscured the hillside, and it was lucky that I even saw it. As we watched, though, the dissipating fog kept revealing other deer.

My decision to leave the spotting scope back in camp was coming back to haunt me. We needed a closer look. There was no choice but to shoulder our packs and trudge up the ridge. Sparse growth, which only a few minutes before was a blessing, now left us in the open without stalking cover. To stay out of sight, we were forced to climb around to the backside of the basin rim leading toward the pass.

Eventually, we were lying in a small opening watching 11 deer, including two bucks. One buck was quite a bit larger than the other. I concentrated on him as they slowly worked their way across the slope. My range finder read 405 yards. I shot my .300 Ultra Mag hundreds of times during the summer to get ready for just this situation. Besides, one of the stadia hairs in my Leupold scope was set exactly on 400 yards. So, I was highly confident that the buck was mine, if it was big enough to shoot. Turning the scope up to 20 power, I could clearly see that the buck was a 3 x 4 with decent eye guards and long tines. After doing some mental gymnastics, I finally decided that it would gross around 100 points, which matched my goal for the Sitka Blacktail.

The bipod was down and the cartridge was in the chamber. All I had to do was slip off the safety, take a deep breath, center the crosshairs, and squeeze the trigger. As I watched through the scope, the buck stepped slightly uphill, giving me a good shot at his front shoulder. The rifle bucked, but I was able to get back to the scope in time to see the buck sliding down the steep slope. The buck never knew what hit him! I had my second buck in my Deer Quest!

The steep slope made walking difficult. When we finally crawled over to where the buck disappeared into the brush, we found its huge body crammed into an alder thicket. It took all of us to pull the buck up to a place where it could be field dressed. I'm not sure what I would have done if I had been there by myself. The mountainside was so steep that Brian had to hold the buck in place to prevent it from sliding back down into the thicket while we boned him out. In a testament to what it takes to survive the harsh winters up North, we were skiving off slabs of fat several inches thick. This buck weighing well over 200 pounds on the hoof was the largest-bodied and fattest blacktail that I have ever killed!

The sun broke through the clouds, burned off the remaining fog, and gave us a chance to finish caping and boning in the warm, gentle breeze. After taking a brief break for lunch and a moment to enjoy the pristine setting, we shouldered our heavy packs and lined out down the mountain. We headed toward the tallest timber we could see, because we had discovered while climbing the hill that walking under the canopy of towering conifers was much easier than fighting through the brush. However, there was a new danger. We had to be extra careful to avoid the bears, since now we were packing fresh meat.

It didn't take us long to find out that the trip down the hill was no more fun than our climb that morning. Don stepped into a hidden hole and twisted his knee so badly that I thought we were going to have to pack him back as well. About halfway down, Wayne's knee also started hurting, and I was feeling renewed pain from knee surgery that I had only weeks before. We were one banged up bunch climbing off that mountain, but our nightmare ended when we arrived at the beach. Rather than make the hike all the way back to the lodge, we collapsed on our packs and called Frank at the lodge to pick us up with the boat. After walking into the lodge, I checked the time and was stunned to see that more than 12 hours had elapsed since we left that morning!

A beer never tasted so good! I was tired to the bone, but strapped on my pack was a rack that was everything I had hoped to find in Alaska. The antlers would later officially score 99-7/8 points. The buck has over 26 inches of mass and an inside spread of almost 15 inches, which, for a Sitka, is decent. With a dark cape, characteristic double-white throat patch, and dark brown, almost black, chevron, the buck would make an attractive addition to my trophy room.

Frank noted that although it was a good buck, better ones were around. He teased me when he said, "If you really want to get a big deer, come on back!" Considering that the B&C All-Time records minimum is 108 points, it says something for the potential on the island. Afognak Island is not known for big bucks, but then much of the island is owned by the ANC and receives little hunting pressure. Kodiak Island, on the other hand, has big bucks, but also has hunting pressure. In addition, Kodiak's Sitka blacktail was hit hard by winter kill a few years ago.

The next morning, my muscles were complaining. I got more of a "real hunt" than I had bargained for, but I still had two unfilled tags left. On the other hand, the prospect of catching some of the acrobatic Cohos or maybe a halibut was also appealing. Fortunately, the weather made my decision easy. The promised storm finally moved in, bringing driving rain and thick clouds covering the ridges where we planned on finding the bucks. Fishing seemed like a great alternative and certainly wasn't a waste of time, since Don was able to catch a big Coho salmon weighing over 18 pounds. We enjoyed the salmon as our main course that night, along with scallops and pasta.

The trip home was an adventure in itself. Because of the terrorist attack on the Twin Towers and the temporary grounding of all air traffic, we were briefly stranded in Kodiak. We were able to get a room at the Best Western for three days while we waited for the airlines to resume flying. We were luckier than some who were forced to stay for days in local churches. The layover gave us time to mend tired bones and fish for saltwater bottom fish and salmon.

In many ways the trip was special. I'll never look at the mount on my wall without remembering panoramic scenery; wild, almost virgin, country, a successful hunt with friends, and our "hike from hell." But it also reminds me of the tragedy and emotions that we all felt on that fateful September day.

One bonus of hunting Sitka blacktail in Alaska is the beautiful country where they roam. This buck proved that they can have huge bodies; this one was the heaviest blacktail ever killed by the author. Even the best mature Sitka may not grow more than three points per side.

Alaska's islands provide quality habitat for Sitka blacktail and breath-taking scenery for the hunter.

Long-range shots from a prone, rock-solid position while being assisted by an experienced spotter are quite predictable. Here, Wayne Long provides advice on windage, while the author makes last-minute adjustments for a shot at his Sitka blacktail.

Gary Sorensen admires his classic 4 x 4 buck. Killed on his first morning's hunt, it shows the results that can be attained with intensive scouting.

Don Causey gave Wayne Long and the author freshwater and saltwater fishing lessons. Our time spent waiting for the airlines to fly after 9/11 wasn't wasted because fishing around Kodiak was terrific!

Typical northern Columbia blacktail habitat. Clearcuts with replanted trees of different ages provide ample cover. Complicated with frequent fog and the ever-present rain, hunting here can be miserable.

California blacktail shot by Gary Sorensen.

Rugged terrain, as well as mixed conifer and dense oak thickets provide Columbia blacktail perfect cover in California. This habitat is decidedly more "hunter friendly" than other blacktail range farther north.

Cody Mallo holds the result of passing his Hunter Safety course and being drawn for one of the hunts donated by Arrow Five Outfitters. This youngster was a trouper while facing all of his first-hunt experiences with enthusiasm. It most likely will not be his last hunt.

Jim Schaafsma and Mitch Besso discuss the origin of the third main beam on the author's buck.

Cody Besso is proud of a buck that may be the best blacktail he'll ever bag, but the memory that will last longest will be this hunt with his father.

Mule
Deer

Nobody's Fool

I'LL MINCE no words—the mule deer is my favorite quarry. I suppose it's partially because I've hunted them since before I was 10 years old and tagged along with my grandfather on December hunts in Colorado. I wasn't much taller than the snow we trudged through, and I didn't carry a rifle, yet some of my fondest hunting memories are rooted in those early hunts.

I hunt mule deer every year now, usually on hunts in several states with radically diverse terrain and habitat. Those hunts have given me a healthy respect for just how difficult it can be to drop a crafty, big-racked mule deer.

According to respected wildlife biologist Valerius Geist, the mule deer is a product of crossbreeding between the whitetail and the blacktail deer species. It seems that North America was first occupied by whitetail deer, which evolved 4 million years ago, soon followed by the evolution of blacktails. Where their ranges overlapped, eventually the mule deer appeared.

Today, the mule deer's range covers a huge region, extending from southern Yukon, Canada, to the southern tip of Baja, Mexico, and from the Midwest prairies to the crest of the Cascade Range. They are found in 17 western states, 5 Canadian provinces, and northern Mexico. This vast range covers incredible diversities of habitat, topography, weather extremes, food and water sources, and elevations. Big muleys are as comfortable in rugged mountains with icy streams, heavy snowfalls, and bitter cold, as they are in Southwest deserts and arid prairies with searing heat and little water.

Wildlife scientists recognize two subspecies of mule deer— Rocky Mountain and desert varieties. They have also divided the desert subspecies into five varieties. The differences between the two subspecies are as sharp as day and night—far more than geographical and topographical distinctions. One major, but disturbing difference is that the Rocky Mountain mule deer is quickly losing ground, and numbers are falling in many areas. On the other hand, over the last 15 years, desert varieties appear to be increasing and herd strengths are improving.

For clarification, in this book I will refer to the Rocky Mountain mule deer as simply "mule deer," the most common and widespread subspecies. Besides, this deer most often comes to mind when people talk about mule deer. The desert variety and subspecies are identified as "desert mule deer."

Rocky Mountain Mule Deer

I was around during the "good old days" when it was easy to see several hundred mule deer a day, and a patient hunter could annually kill bucks with sweeping trophy racks. Unfortunately, most modern hunters now see antlers like that only in their sweetest dreams. In those golden days, mule deer were commonly derided as the whitetail's dumb cousin. Man, have times changed!

Today, we are witnessing a decline of mule deer populations so severe that it would have been unimaginable in the late '50s. Compounding the problem are rapidly evolving behavioral changes. The mule deer we hunt today is wary, elusive, and not the same naïve mule deer we hunted in the 1950s. What's remarkable to me is that the change occurred within only a few decades.

I believe there are several explanations for why hunters are finding it increasingly difficult to kill big mule deer bucks. First, many historical ranges that supported big bucks only a few decades ago have changed for the worse, perhaps forever. Encroaching civilization has had a terrible impact on mule deer, which are by nature solitary creatures that don't fare well when forced to compete with housing developments, five-acre ranchettes, new roads, agricultural land uses, and the hustle and bustle of humans.

Second, mule deer are losing the competition for remaining habitat to a steady encroachment of whitetail deer. Wildlife biologists have found that mule deer ranges shrink wherever they overlap ranges used by whitetails. These overlaps most often take place in the low-elevation prairies, fields, and creek bottoms that mule deer depend on for winter range and where whitetails live year-round.

The reasons are complicated, but Valerius Geist maintains that hybridization between whitetail and mule deer is the ultimate threat that could lead to extinction of mule deer over much of their historical range. There is no doubt that mule deer range is shrinking even in their former strongholds of Montana, western Idaho, and Wyoming.

It's not a matter of competition in the traditional sense because nature dictates that mule deer and whitetails generally seek different habitat, terrain, and cover. Whitetails prefer thick cover and have a natural wariness that make it possible for young bucks to survive heavy hunting pressure long enough to develop large racks. Mule deer generally prefer more open terrain and lack the whitetails' inherent wariness; thus, many of the young bucks are cropped long before they are old enough to develop trophy antlers. Several states are trying to reduce the impact on young bucks by reducing mule deer general hunting seasons, increasing doe-only permits, and restricting buck kills to deer with three-point antler minimums. The long-range success of these management strategies is still an unknown.

Mule deer bucks, according to Geist's studies, have difficulty breeding whitetail does, which easily outmaneuver slower, less aggressive mule deer bucks. Whitetail bucks, on the other hand, are faster than mule deer does, and they successfully breed them. The result is a loss of a breeding mule deer doe and the negative long-term impact that this has on the mule deer population. There is a resulting decrease in pure-bred mule deer fawns and a downward spiral for overall mule deer populations. Biologists have found that excessively cropping young bucks and herd reduction through hybridization occur most often in low, rolling country. They also found that where terrain is steep and rugged, young mule deer bucks better survive hunting seasons and muley does more easily evade whitetail bucks.

The third reason why I suspect that it has become increasingly difficult to kill a big mule deer is that many states are scheduling deer hunting seasons and imposing restrictions aimed solely at conserving declining herd populations, tipping the odds in favor of the big bucks. Often, general deer seasons are closed during the best hunting periods. Only a few states still offer mule deer hunting during the rut, and many of those hunts are allocated on a public drawing basis for a very limited number of permits.

The main reasons that I believe fewer big bucks are now being taken is that big old muley bucks now rival whitetails for wariness and elusiveness. Big western muley bucks have simply adapted to heavy hunting pressure, as did their eastern whitetail cousins eons earlier. Historically, a spooked mule deer headed for fairly open high ground where it could use its bouncy, ground-eating stott, decent eyesight, and excellent hearing to full advantage. A mule deer's instinct is to locate danger and maintain a safe distance from it. This is an instinct that works better against coyotes and cougars than .300 Winchester magnums with bipod rests. It's also an instinct that I suspect is accelerating an evolutionary change in mule deer behavior. Many mule deer are now as likely to remain icy cool and composed under hunting pressure as they are to bolt in panic. My explanation is that the bucks that prefer open-country flight to hunkering coolly in the pucker brush are being eliminated from the gene pool. The buck that hides is the buck that survives to breed. These days, a big muley buck caught in close quarters is as likely as a whitetail to freeze, hunker down, and let the hunter walk by. When he does explode from cover, he's not likely to hesitate.

Some things about mule deer haven't changed, though. A mature buck that has survived more than a half-dozen hunting seasons is much warier than a juvenile. Big bucks will bed on vantage points where they can see or hear approaching predators and will move out at the first hint of danger. When spooked or pushed by hunting pressure, they simply will clear out of the country. Trophy-class bucks are creatures of the high country and prefer space between themselves and a threat. I've watched spooked bucks run for miles, and wise old bucks head to sanctuaries as far as possible from roads.

I would venture to say that the three most successful hunting techniques for killing a big mule deer are to spot and stalk, still-hunt, or try to drive them. Of the three, I feel that your chances are infinitely better by trying to set up high and spot an unspooked buck at long distance. It provides ample time to evaluate trophy potential, to watch the buck bed, and mark the spot before stalking within shooting distance. This is a game of high-power optics and patience. Often, I see quite a few deer before finding a possible trophy. One of the problems with long-range spotting is that big deer typically hold in thick cover during the day and only venture out in the fringes of light when there's little time left for a stalk.

Spotting and stalking was the favorite hunting technique for my son, Mark, and me for years on our Idaho hunts. We hunted a tight little area covering less than 1.5 square miles, and we would stay there for more than a week—sitting on the same lookouts watching and waiting for our break. It was mountain country with dense conifer stands, interspersed with aspen groves, rugged rock outcroppings, and slides. In other words, perfect habitat for holding a big buck. In five years, we never missed seeing at least one trophy buck, and we killed two B&C candidates.

One hunt stands out in my mind as an example of what hunting prime big buck country with patience can produce. We had hunted for over a week, and the last few days of the season were fast approaching. Finally, just before dark, we spotted a good buck chasing several does high on a ridge above our lookouts. That night over dinner, Mark told me that he wanted to try to find that buck the next day.

After only a few hours of sleep, we were humping it up the steep ridge in the inky darkness. A skiff of slippery snow made walking difficult, and by the time I reached our lower lookout, I was bushed. Mark volunteered to push on to the upper lookout. I dumped my pack, settled in, and waited for light. It was barely light enough to see through my binoculars when I spotted the damnedest buck I had ever seen. I didn't need a second look. I threw my gear in my pack and took off as fast as I could to the upper lookout.

When I arrived, Mark's spotting scope was pointed into the basin, and he was gone! Obviously, he had also seen the big buck. There wasn't much I could do but wait and watch. I soon spotted the buck from the night before higher on the ridge and alone. I suspect that the big buck had kicked his butt during the night and stolen his does. I lost interest in this buck when I relocated the 40-inch monster that I had seen from the lower lookout, now on the hillside less than 800 yards away. I sat down to watch the show.

After five minutes of intense glassing, I still hadn't located Mark and was beginning to get concerned when I saw him climbing back out of the basin toward me. Soon, he was sitting behind the scope. He'd broken off the stalk, he said, after losing sight of the buck and does in the folds and cuts of the hill. Not wanting to spook the super trophy, he had decided to return to get another fix on its position. As the sun rose, the does were slowly leading him toward the timber. He was less than 50 yards from cover when Mark charged back down the slope. Minutes passed like hours, and the buck was only a few steps away from disappearing into the timber when a shot rang out. He didn't connect, but for both of us it was the highlight of our hunt that year. It was even more exciting than the B&C buck Mark shot the next day. Episodes like this cement my faith in spotting and stalking big mule deer. It was just bad luck that kept that 40-inch buck off Mark's trophy room wall.

The second most successful hunting technique is still-hunting, especially if the terrain includes rimrock, which is a favorite bedding area for a big buck. Muleys tend to pick elevated beds where they are protected by rock behind them and a thin screen of brush in front. A hunter slowly picking his way along the face of rimrock, while taking plenty of breaks to glass, is frequently rewarded with venison.

Drives also account for their share of big bucks, but I believe that most old mossyhorns give drivers the slip. I've watched several drives from distant vantage points as big bucks craftily evaded the hunters. Still, enough hunters have killed trophies using this technique that it's a tactic that can't be ignored. I do think, however, that this technique was more productive years ago before big bucks learned to hold still and stay cool.

With one exception, mule deer hunters should forget that favorite whitetail hunting technique of patterning bucks and sitting in a stand. Sometimes it is possible to catch them coming off an alfalfa field. In my experience, though, the older, bigger bucks leave far before first light or arrive after dark.

There are very few mule deer hunters with more than one big buck to their credit (eliminating all except those that are incredibly lucky) who don't admire and respect trophy-class mule deer for the challenge they pose. These tough, wary, big game animals have earned a special place in the hearts of those of us who have chased big bucks for years.

Desert Mule Deer

The desert muley is found in a number of states, including the extreme southern portions of California, Arizona, and New Mexico, as well as the Trans Pecos region of Texas. They also are found in Baja, California, as well as the Mexican states of Sonora, Chihuahua, and Coahuila. Desert muleys are divided into five subspecies and are scattered over such a wide geographic area that they display regional variance in physical size and coloration.

In recent seasons, the largest desert mule deer bucks are being killed in Sonora. These bucks typically have smaller bodies than their northern cousins, but often carry very wide, typical racks that score high.

Desert deer inhabit desert and arid regions, an area of harsh conditions and limited water sources. Deer have adapted to these conditions and get most of their water requirements from eating water-retaining forage and succulents. They are also masters at finding seeps and natural sources of water. Apparently, the forage is also very high in nutrients, because I don't believe that I have ever seen a desert mule deer in poor condition.

It's almost always a revelation to first-time desert mule deer hunters when they discover that the deer's home is on the desert floor, or perhaps in the nearby low, rolling hills, and not the highest accessible elevations. This, then, somewhat dictates how they are hunted. Over most of their range, spot-and-stalk hunting is not possible because there is little elevation to give hunters a vantage point that allows them to glass a lot of ground. Where the terrain allows, spot-and-stalk tactics may be effective, but the odds are stacked against the hunter. Spotting a buck is just the first problem. A stalk to find him again in a sea of often featureless desert foliage, and then closing in to get the shot, is more of a challenge than many hunters can handle.

The most common and successful desert mule deer hunting techniques are tracking or riding on a vehicle with an elevated seat to see over the brush. Of these two, tracking is my favorite because you are one-on-one with the buck, challenging it on its own turf. Everything is stacked in the buck's favor. Until you have seen a good Mexican tracker follow a track, you have no grasp of the skill it takes to be successful. It is truly amazing to watch. This is where a lot of mistakes are made, because more often than not, the trophy potential of the buck has to be sized up and passed or shot in a split second. Besides, a buck always looks bigger running away.

This is probably why many hunters pass up tracking in favor of road hunting. Many good bucks are shot by hunters driving ranch roads in trucks equipped with elevated racks and seats that allow them to see over the dense desert foliage. Generally, the high seats give hunters more time to evaluate the buck and make a good decision. Perhaps the biggest advantage to this technique is that hunters cover a lot of country. Since the population density of mule deer in the desert is generally very low, this is probably the most productive way to kill a good buck.

I really enjoy hunting the desert mule deer for several reasons. One reason is that the best hunting occurs in late December and January when normally it's raining in Oregon. These hunts give me a chance to travel to country highlighted by sunshine and cloudless, warm days. Many people visualize the desert as a foreboding, arid, and faceless land. I find the desert beautiful, especially when there's ample moisture and it comes alive with color—flowers crowning plants normally covered in thorns, stickers, and spines.

I have been on 10 desert mule deer hunts. With luck and good guides, I have tagged seven bucks, with four carrying spreads that exceeded 30 inches. I've also been in on the kill of two other big bucks in Sonora, a Mexican state with enormous trophy potential.

I also believe that I have been luckier than most hunters who venture to Mexico. Hunter success is normally around 20 to 25 percent and anything more is gravy. If my experience is any guide, this is the place for someone interested in killing bucks with big, typical antlers. It is not, however, the place to see one of the huge, nontypical bucks sometimes found further north. Older desert mule deer bucks will often throw kickers, but their racks will typically be massive, rather than growing many long, extra tines.

My best desert mule deer buck is an 8 x 11, 34-inch buck, with almost 6-inch bases. I killed this buck in 1999 while hunting with German Rivas. Without a doubt, that buck is the highlight of my hunts in Sonora. However, at the other extreme, on a different hunt I killed another 30-incher that was my biggest disappointment.

On that hunt, I had the chance to shoot a huge typical buck standing broadside at less than 250 yards. The problem was that he had us pegged and he was getting ready to depart—rapidly! I had one chance for an offhand shot, and I just plain overshot him. Even though I didn't have a long look, it was enough time to convince me that the buck may have scored over 210 points!

Two days later, my guide and I were back. The rut was raging, and there was a chance that the buck would return to his harem.

We had found his does in some low hills and were headed toward them, but before we got there, we jumped another buck that looked high, wide, and heavy. I whacked him. When I walked up to the downed buck my enthusiasm faded. He was only a 3 x 3, slightly over 30-inches wide, with 5-1/2 inch bases and G-2s that were over 19-1/2 inches long. He was a good buck, but I couldn't grow the fourth points on the rack that are needed for a high score. Such are the risks of hunting desert mule deer. Snap shots are often necessary, sometimes with good results, sometimes not. Often, this is when hunters unhappily learn the true meaning of "ground shrinkage."

God has apparently reserved a special place in His Kingdom for the mule deer! It must be true because humans aren't smart enough to commercially raise the mule deer, although many game ranches successfully raise whitetail and elk. You can be confident when you see a beautiful mule deer mount that it wasn't raised and shot behind a ranch's game fence. Rather, it was harvested as a result of the hunter's skill and probably taken in some of the most beautiful country this continent has to offer. Come to think of it, that is probably God's gift to us!

Magic
on Santa Rosa Island

OUTFITTER Gordon Long, hunter Bob George, and I were driving along a rim overlooking the beautiful Pacific Ocean cupped into the shoreline hundreds of feet below us. A two-masted schooner was anchored in the lagoon, and I could barely see two swimmers cooling off in the rolling waves. It was the first week in September, and a cool marine breeze was blowing up the ridge keeping us quite comfortable on top. The scene was a long way from the typical semi-arid, rock-and-sage mule deer country that most of us envision in our hunting dreams.

As we drove along the edge above the ocean, Bob spun his story about the 205-point buck he killed the year before. He had collected his trophy in one of the most unique spots in the West for record-book mule deer hunting. We were on Santa Rosa Island in the Channel Island group northwest of Los Angeles. I had hunted there before, and I had faith that big bucks there were still around—maybe even bigger than Bob's exceptional trophy!

Gordy turned the truck off a short grade as we approached Clapp Springs. The sun was high overhead, and I expected to spot deer lying in the shade of the deep gorge that dropped away to our right. As we approached, a small buck busted out of the head of the gorge and was doing his best to put some distance between us. It took only a second to recognize that he wasn't what we wanted. I started to relax when suddenly several more deer came pouring out of the bottom of the gorge.

My eyes focused on the biggest buck—partly because he had a cluster of extra points. Some hunters call these "trash" points, but to me they are "treasures." Unfortunately, it was past noon, and by mutual agreement, it was now Bob's turn to shoot.

"There goes a nontypical," I blurted out. "Hurry!"

But there was no shot!

Imagine hunting in country where there wouldn't be an immediate response to seeing a good nontypical getting away. I was glued to my binoculars and had no idea that Gordy and Bob, instead of passing on the buck as I thought, were waiting for it to reappear from a cut. Just as it popped into view and cleared the brush, Bob's rifle thundered. The buck crumbled as if he'd been hit by lightening. A .300 Winchester has that effect on deer.

Unfortunately, it didn't stay where it dropped. The dead deer slid down the steep slope before cramming into scrub brush and rocks in the bottom. We were all grunting and groaning while we manhandled the big buck up to the trail. The buck's 6 x 12 rack wasn't wide, but he had two drop points off his right main beam, and one drop point had an extra kicker. The points weren't long, but the velvet made them look massive and impressive. I was envious, not only because nontypical bucks are one of my weaknesses, but also because this buck had character.

Knives slashed and cameras flashed, and within an hour we had the buck field dressed, packed into the truck, and were heading west toward Black Mountain. For the rest of the afternoon it seemed that every canyon held more deer—a buck on the far hillside or a group of bachelors running together. That night I reviewed my notes and found that we had seen 62 bucks, including groups of as many as 10. It was one of those days that most of us can only dream about. Such is the potential of hunting on Santa Rosa Island. Not only are there a lot of deer, but as the two bucks hanging on the meat pole in camp proved, there are some dandies! Rod Fogle tagged a 4 x 4 that morning that stretched the tape to 34 inches.

Wayne Long and his son, Gordon, owners of Multiple Use Managers (MUM), have been leaders in private land big game management for years. Certainly, their cornerstone operation is on Santa Rosa Island, off the California coast near Santa Barbara.

The Pacific Ocean provides a unique background for the author's last-minute mule deer buck. The Kaibab strain produces some very large trophies on Santa Rosa Island.

This proximity to major cities leads most clients to be pleasantly surprised upon landing on the island. The 30 miles of water between the island and mainland is a transition for people to step back in time to when the West was really wild! The ranch started as a land grant from the Mexican government, and its history is replete with shootings and mystery. Before that, it was the land of the Chumash Indians, long ago extinct. Their artifacts and village remnants are still subjects of interest. Since 1908, the ranch has been under the control of the Park Service and the Channel Islands National Park and is now changing from private to public ownership.

Between 1903 and 1997, Santa Rosa Island was an operating cattle ranch run by Vail & Vickers Company. In 1997 the last Mexican cowboy and cow left the island, a bureaucratic change that, in my mind, is just another sacrifice to the narrow "vision" of the National Park Service. When the cowboys and cows left, Americans lost yet another small part of our Western heritage along with leather lariats, wild horses, and tough men. The Park Ranger's next target is the outstanding hunting found on the island.

Roosevelt elk and Kaibab mule deer were introduced to the huge 85-square-mile island after the turn of the century, and they have prospered under careful management, the last 21 years under MUM's guidance. Most avid sportsmen have heard about the island's fantastic elk hunting, but the mule deer are the "story behind the story." These deer evolved from the Kaibab gene pool, so it's no surprise that many bucks carry wide, massive racks, and some have those high-scoring G-4s that made the Kaibab famous. The isolated island has provided a platform for demonstrating the strengths of combining professional wildlife management with enlightened private landowner operations.

What is the status of hunting on the island? Certainly, the story has changed several times, but the one constant is that hunting and introduced wildlife are being phased out. Just a few years ago, it was questionable if hunting would continue beyond 1998. Now, the public should be hunting Santa Rosa until 2011. The management plan, however, is up for review every five years. Essentially, by 2008, the present mule deer and elk population levels must be reduced by 50 percent, and all will be gone in 2011. After that, all that will remain on the island will be a few park rangers, their posies, and of course, their satellite dish.

Until then MUM will continue to outfit deer and elk hunts. All hunts are conducted on a 2 x 1 guided basis. Hunts are four-day events including one-half days on both ends to allow for flight service between the mainland and the island. They consistently produce a 100 percent hunter success. Several years ago, during my first island hunt, I saw eight bucks that I felt were between 29 and 32 inches wide. The memory of those hat-rack bucks is the reason I selected Santa Rosa as one of the "must do" hunts for mule deer in my "triple-double" project.

I wasn't disappointed! By noon on the second day, Gordy, Bob, and I had spotted and passed on more than 100 bucks. This included the 24 bucks we saw in only a few hours after we arrived by plane. On that first night, after seeing how many big deer were available, I promised myself that I would hold out for one of the

These Roosevelt elk sheds were found while hunting mule deer.

trophies that I knew roamed these hills. I'll admit, though, during the next few days, it was tough to pass on the half-dozen bucks that exceeded my self-imposed "triple-double" target of 180 points.

For example, one morning there were two bucks we watched feed with three other deer along a side hill about 250 yards away. One buck was noticeably bigger than the other. In the spotting scope, I could see the burrs sprouting on the base of his rack, but I didn't need the big scope to see that he carried four long tines on each side. I guessed that his G-4s were well over 9 inches, certainly adequate to make the grade in that department. I was also impressed with its mass. The only negative was that the main beams were only 23 inches long—a little short for a topflight score. Gordy and I both agreed that the buck would score in the low 180s, a quality buck, but still not quite what I hoped to find. We turned our back and kept hunting.

The Search Continues—A New Meaning

After lunch, we were on the move again. To be honest, I wasn't paying attention, that is, until I saw a buck and doe in the bottom of a canyon. Raising my glasses, I confirmed that the buck's rack

Gordy Long takes advantage of a much needed break during lunch. A warm breeze and spectacular beach scenery are major differences between Santa Rosa hunts and other typical mule deer hunts.

was mediocre. Just as I dropped the binoculars, however, I saw four other bucks break out of a side canyon, running directly toward the other deer.

One was a keeper—he was wide, with very deep forks and a super frame! We started the stalk, crossing a half-mile of plateau to the edge of the canyon. I mentally started my check-off list: focus on the body, slip off the safety, and take my time. These routines have stood the test of time in my hunting over the years. I cranked up the variable magnification on my rifle scope to 20 power because I expected that when we peeked over the edge, the buck would run toward the far canyon wall. I anticipated a shot of less than 400 yards with plenty of time to aim as the buck picked his way up the steep slope. I was ready!

We neared the rim when Gordy suddenly stopped and threw up his glasses. In a side draw less than 100 yards away, a 24-incher had us nailed! We backed off and dropped behind the rim before slowly creeping forward. As we stuck our heads over, the small buck and four others, including the shooter, were watching us. At first, they only stared, giving me time to raise my rifle and look offhand.

I whispered, "Is he big enough?"

Gordy's response was emphatic, "You bet!"

The bucks were nervous and began to move up the slope. I slipped the safety off, spun the scope power down, centered the buck in the crosshairs, and squeezed. The damned thing didn't shoot! Looking down, I immediately saw the problem—I hadn't flipped the safety all the way off on the Model 70. It was caught in the middle position between safe and fire and only took a second to correct, but unfortunately, I was starting to get frantic.

Again, I raised the rifle, while asking, "Is he the last one?"

"Yes," Gordy shot back.

I was about to try again, but something didn't look quite right. Thankfully, I took the time to swing farther to the left, and there was another buck pulling up the rear. By now, they were 250 yards off and making tracks in those ground-eating bounds. The buck was quartering away. I pulled ahead and squeezed the trigger.

I lost sight of the deer in the recoil and was shoving another round into the chamber when Gordy's cry of "You got him!" registered in my brain. By the time I found him again in the scope, all I could see was the top of his rack bobbing behind a small rise. Then he was gone!

We all started talking at once. The buck was hit hard, "blowing him sideways," as Bob described what he saw in his glasses. He said that it was the first time he had ever seen a buck hit that hard and keep running. They were both confident that we would find him piled up behind the rise. Still, I wasn't going to rest until I was standing over his body.

We took off running down into the draw and up the other side. At the top, I was breathing so hard I sounded like a steam engine. We walked directly to the spot where I had hit the buck and found a small sliver of fat and a little blood. I was concerned that there was no blood trail! We spread out, walking in the general direction the buck had taken. After 10 minutes, it was plainly evident that the buck didn't die, and now we were looking for an injured, smart old buck. Bob dropped into the deep gorge where we thought the buck had headed, hoping to cut him off and turn him back toward us.

A doe broke out of the bottom and got my heart pounding before I realized that it wasn't "my buck." A sick feeling began to grow in the pit of my stomach. I have wounded only two bucks that got away in my half century of hunting. I still remember and think about those debacles, and I didn't want to go through it again.

I plopped down for some serious glassing. He had to be there, somewhere! I started searching at the far end of the ravine and was slowly working back. Suddenly, I found him—standing looking back over his butt at us about a half-mile away. There was no doubt about that rack. Taking my eyes away from the binoculars, I yelled, "There he is!"

I needed to keep track of the buck because Gordy was still climbing up the backside of the ridge and wouldn't be able to see it. When I found him again, the buck was already moving, not running, just slowly working his way toward a fence line. I watched him cross the fence and disappear behind a ridge. I hoped that once we were out of sight (and since we didn't push him) the buck would lie down. I decided to wait for Gordy and Bob. It took Bob over a half-hour to climb back out of the canyon and catch up to us at the truck.

It gave me plenty of time to think, and I was getting sicker by the minute. We drove to the fence to see if we could pick up tracks and found a small pool of blood where the buck had stood watching me, but that was the only evidence that this wasn't just a nightmare. The grass was knee high in places, but even though we looked carefully, we couldn't see any sign of where he had passed.

It was now 3:00 p.m., and there was plenty of daylight left. Frankly, I thought that we would jump the buck somewhere on top. Gordy, on the other hand, thought that we would find him down by a small creek in Arlington Canyon about a mile west. We spread out and walked out the logical hiding places, including both sides of the creek. Country that looked from the top to be fairly smooth was in actuality cut with dozens of small erosion gullies, some several feet deep and others impassable—all deep enough to swallow a buck that was trying to hide. Six hours later, darkness stopped our search without our finding a sign of the buck. It was a long, quiet ride back to camp that night. It didn't help my disposition when the guys told me that they thought the buck had a spread of between 32 and 34 inches. But at that point, all I cared about was finding the buck and putting an end to the saga. Even Jeanne Munger's terrific meal couldn't make me feel better that night.

At dawn we were joined by six other hunters and guides from camp. They generously took some of their best hunting time left to help me find the wounded buck. It's hard to find folks like that, but that's the quality of people you find in hunting camps. When we stepped out of the trucks, it was so foggy I could barely make out detail 300 yards away.

The night before, on their way back to camp, one of the other hunting parties had spotted what they described as a 32-inch buck in the trees not far above the corrals in Arlington Canyon. That's where we started. I took the high ground, hoping to get a long shot should he get up on the far side or bump out from one of the drivers paralleling the side hill. The drive rousted a lot of deer from the trees, but not the one we were hoping to find. When we finally stopped, we reluctantly agreed that if "my buck" was healthy enough to cover the several miles from where I last saw him, he probably would be even farther away by now. We turned back, spread out again, and started walking the slopes. One guide did find a small glob of fat near the fence, but that was it! There was no other sign, no trail, or spots of blood on the grass blades— nothing. At times, we were down on our knees searching for sign. It was heartbreaking.

It was after 10:00 a.m. when the other guides gathered up their clients and headed off to fill their remaining tags. We were now on our own, but Gordy and Bob were still game to help me search. The topography created plenty of hiding spots in a network of shallow and deep gullies, dips and pockets, smooth slopes and rugged rimrock, sunlit grass slopes and shaded creek banks. I suspected that when we found the buck, he would be dead.

That afternoon we stopped for a tailgate lunch on a high bluff overlooking the blue ocean and white surf crashing on the rocks below us. We piled our sliced pork roast sandwiches high with all the goodies and tried to relax. We all needed rest and, after eating, settled in for a short catnap. I had just dropped off when I heard Gordy say, "Come here and look at this."

At the far end of the beach there were several ledges of rock extending nearly 50 yards out into the surf. On the far end of the farthest ledge, a small buck was standing in the water, facing into the wind, with the surf splashing on him. None of us had ever seen anything like this, nor did we understand what the buck was doing, but it was one of the highlights etched in my mind. Unfortunately, he was too far away to photograph. It was impossible to tell how long he had been standing there, but we watched for about two minutes until he turned and gingerly worked his way back over the rocks to the beach and out of sight.

We put in the rest of the day walking and looking for sign, but still didn't turn up a clue of where "my buck" had disappeared. We covered the full length of both sides of Arlington Canyon, some five miles to the ocean. After we had eliminated the main canyon, we worked back to where we had first located the buck and then zigzagged back and forth across the side hills. I have no idea how many miles we put in that day, but my companions never complained.

It would be an understatement to say that I was depressed the next morning when I climbed aboard the plane for the flight out. As I packed to leave, I had asked the guides to watch for scavenger birds circling the area where I shot the buck. There was always a chance that they would find the downed animal while hunting with other clients. Over the next several months, I checked in from time to time, but by mid-November there was still no sign of the buck.

Now I had a decision to make. Earlier that spring, I had drawn one of the limited and highly coveted Nevada late-hunt deer tags. However, the Santa Rosa buck still weighed heavily on my mind, and in the end I decided to cancel my planned Nevada hunt. It would mean "eating" my tag and sacrificing my accumulated bonus points and the best chance I might ever have to kill one of the bucks that has made Nevada famous. Thankfully, when I talked with Wayne, I was able to make arrangements to return to Santa Rosa and continue my search for the buck.

Back At It Again

Our plane banked over Santa Rosa's dirt landing field on November 14, my birthday. Wayne and the guides were waiting in pickups to help pack my gear and that of the other hunters to the ranch. Just after landing, one of the guides, Jim Settle, brought me good news. Only a few days earlier, while guiding an elk hunter, he had spotted a pile of bones lying on Arlington's grassy slopes. He

Greg Amaral holds his magnificent buck, one of several he has killed on Santa Rosa Island.

thought that it would be difficult to describe where the bones were, since they were partially hidden in the deep grass. It was music to my ears when Jimmy agreed to show me the spot.

After a few minutes of getting organized and settling into my room, I went to their range to check my rifle zero. It was lucky that I checked because I couldn't touch the paper target. One of my scope mounts had loosened. After securing it again and cranking off a couple of verification rounds, there was still time to drive to Arlington Canyon for the last few hours of daylight.

The good news is we found the bones. The bad news is that they turned out to be the remains of a cow elk. The walk back to the truck was filled with the same bad memories, unanswered questions, and doubts that I carried out of this gully months earlier. Suddenly, I was jarred back to reality by the sight of a limping buck less than a quarter-mile away crossing a shallow gully. I hoped that Lady Luck was smiling again.

By quietly ducking into the tucks and folds in the rolling hillside, we were able to sneak in close, to less than 75 yards. We didn't need the spotting scope to see that it wasn't the buck I had wounded. This rack was decidedly narrower, and the tines were shorter, although the clean 4 x 4 would have easily scored above 175 points. The buck's injuries were apparently from rutting battles resulting in an ugly gash that laid open almost the full length of his left jaw. He also apparently had been gored in the gut, because he couldn't go far before he had to lie down. Jimmy and I agreed to allow nature to dictate his fate.

The next morning, Wayne and I returned to Arlington Canyon for one last attempt. My notes verified that we had already spent over 95 man hours searching for the buck, not counting the guides' time spent over the last several months. We agreed that we'd made an honest effort, and if we hadn't found him by noon, we would give up and hunt another buck. All too soon, noon came and went without any sign of the great buck.

To turn away and finally admit that I was whipped was one of the more difficult things I've had to do in my hunting career. I now believe that I must have nicked him high in the hip, thus the fat and almost no blood. To this day I second guess myself—what would have happened if I had slipped the safety off cleanly the first time? Should I have passed on the running shot, hoping that the buck would give me a standing shot at possibly 500 yards as he climbed the slope? Or, rather than waiting for Gordy and Bob, should I have sprinted back to the truck and tried to cut the buck off? I'll never know, and now I have to live with the consequences. But I don't have to like it!

Starting Over

After a quick lunch at camp, Wayne and I were on our way to an area west of Old Ranch House Canyon to look for a buck two other guides had located only days before. Jimmy told me that he was a dandy. Our camp taxidermist and part-time guide, Rod Rust, watched the buck for over one-half hour on two different evenings and thought that he might score as much as 200 points! We weren't making much progress in getting there—we couldn't go one-half mile without bumping into another bunch of deer. We didn't dare just pass them without looking, and the frequent stops were taking big bites out of my hunting time.

One herd of at least 30 deer was preoccupied with the rut, including the eight bucks that were racing about. We scoped out each buck, but couldn't find one that would make the grade. The antlers of one buck were exceptionally tall, with G-2s that had to be over 18 inches. It had everything, except for one major flaw— his inside spread couldn't have been over 21 inches. It's hard to make up those five to seven points lost in a score. Besides, we had a 200-point buck out there somewhere!

Shortly after we left that buck we were overlooking a chunk of ground known as the Honey Hole. It's a spot favored by many of the guides because of the bucks they had killed there in the past. With our glasses and spotting scopes, we carefully dissected the area tree by tree until full dark, but never saw the big buck.

The next morning we were out well before daylight, groping through a ground fog that was socked in so tight we couldn't see 100 yards. We hoped that the fog would be gone up higher, but when we stopped near the Honey Hole, we still couldn't see. We started walking under cover of the heavy fog trying to slip into a vantage point where Wayne said that we could see well later in the morning. We walked slowly and tried to be as quiet as possible, but every little noise seemed to carry into the fog like a gunshot. Several elk crashed off into the mist, and I was worried that they might push everything out of the country. I was concentrating on carefully placing my next step when I just about ran into Wayne's back when he stopped.

It was almost 8:30 a.m. before the fog began to lift. The waves of fog rolled up the ridge at us, turning the far slope into a game board of now-you-see-deer, now-you-don't. As blankets of fog rolled across the hill, feeding deer would seem to materialize, then vaporize. Suddenly, not 30 yards below us, a buck broke out of the creek bottom heading downstream in hot pursuit of a doe. As he rounded a bend, I could see that he was a good one, but not even close to the 200 pointer that we hoped was bedded somewhere across from us. I passed. We kept seeing deer long after the fog lifted, but the big buck had apparently pulled out of the Honey Hole.

We decided to hunt toward Clapp Springs. Deer were now out feeding on the sunny hillsides after the fog's penetrating chill wore off. By early afternoon, we had worked our way to the south side of La Hoya Canyon. The bucks were now bedded, and we paid particular attention while glassing to the shady sides of the trees and other likely bedding spots. Wayne broke the silence with, "There's a good buck!" pointing downhill to a creek at the base of the ridge.

Despite his careful directions, it seemed to take me forever to pick out the buck. As so often happens, when I finally spotted him, I wondered why I hadn't seen him earlier. He was bedded along the creek in the shade of an oxbow bluff carved out by spring runoff. It was a big buck and certainly deserved a closer look in my spotting scope! I was soon thinking about shooting, when two unseen does got up and started down the creek. The buck jumped up and followed. They weren't spooked—it was just time to leave.

Wayne and I were scrambling along the rim above the creek trying to catch up. We caught glimpses of the deer as they dodged in and out of the brush and walked along the creek. Thirty minutes later we figured that we were finally ahead of the deer and set up for an ambush. Immediately, we spotted another buck and a doe bedded under trees less than a hundred yards from our hiding place.

Our luck soured when a puff of wind hit us in the back. In a flash, the bedded deer were up and moving. Much to our amazement, the two were soon joined by nine more deer that had been scattered along the creek. One of the last bucks climbing out of the drainage was the one we'd been shadowing from the oxbow. He gave me plenty of time to carefully look him over. In fact, we were able to parallel him for a while to glass from different angles. He was close, but not quite what I was looking for. It was getting monotonous, but we were once again hiking back empty-handed.

Cutting It Close

I lost count of how many bucks we glassed and passed. All too soon, it was my last evening! Wayne had to stay in camp to get ready to pull out the next morning, so Will Wooley jumped into the truck with me. Will had been raised on Santa Rosa Island and knew it like the back of his hand. I would have been happy to take any advice he had to offer, but I wasn't surprised when Arlington Canyon was mentioned. Despite everything, I hadn't given up hope. At the last moment, instead of dropping into Arlington, Will decided to try another canyon to the west called Soledad Canyon. This canyon was made famous years earlier by an archeologist named Orr, whose camp was located at the mouth of the canyon.

As we approached, we could see a bank of fog creeping toward us across San Miguel Passage. By the time we reached the bluff above the beach, the fog was already filtering the sun's rays, making it difficult to glass. Still, it didn't take long to spot a buck feeding not far from the beach. I got out my spotting scope and adjusted it to 20 power. The low magnification helped, but the fog was still

Anne Chisum proudly shows the 30-inch buck she dreamed
of finding on Santa Rosa Island.

causing me fits. I could see well enough to know that it was a great
buck! I figured him at 34-inches wide, with decent mass and great
fronts. He even had a 4- or 5-inch kicker coming off the right G-2.
One moment I thought that I could see good G-3s and the next, I
wasn't sure. It finally dawned on me that these tines were not crabbed
off, but divided fairly low and grew close to the G-2s, creating the
false impression that they were short.

It only took a few moments for me to decide that this was the
buck I wanted. This was my last mule deer hunt in my Deer
Quest, and it was almost over. He was less than 500 yards away. I
could have cut the distance to a point-blank shot of less than 300
yards by crawling behind the ridge, but I was reluctant to lose
sight of the buck. I was also afraid that by the time I skirted the
ridge, the thick fog might move in and make the shot even more
difficult. I certainly didn't want to risk another bad shot! It occurred
to me that I still had a couple hours to hunt in the morning before
the plane arrived. We backed out and made plans to return at first

light for the buck. During the drive back to camp, my spirits were higher than they had been in a long time.

The plan was simple. We would leave camp before dawn and be in position when the sun peaked out. We hoped we would find the buck somewhere near the mouth of the canyon, not far from where we left him feeding. It seemed foolproof, but as with many plans this one changed just before we left camp. Will had to stay in camp to help get the meat ready to ship out, and Jimmy agreed to join me. It would be a matter of either finding the buck quickly, or coming back to camp skunked. There wasn't time for anything else.

Then I made a serious mistake!

Jimmy and I were in such a hurry to switch our gear from one truck to the other that I failed to talk with him about where we were headed. Consequently, we took the wrong road because Jimmy thought that we had spotted the buck in an entirely different canyon. After getting back on track, we were fairly skimming over the ruts. Still, we did stop for a moment to glass a good nontypical bedded on a small rise, but left quickly because time was wasting. We had to be back to the ranch by 9:30 a.m., and the return drive would take nearly an hour—leaving us less than an hour of hunting.

Soon we were overlooking the beach and mouth of the canyon above Orr's Camp. Jimmy and I had no more than pulled up when we spotted two does and a small buck at the top of a ridge to the east. The buck had his nose on the ground chasing one of the does. Suddenly, a much bigger buck came running over the ridge, cut out the doe and pushed her back out of sight. I only had a glimpse before he disappeared, but it looked like the buck from the night before. Our stalk had just started when suddenly the buck and doe appeared while streaking toward a ravine leading to the beach. I knew that if he made it that far we would never see him again. It was now or never. I pulled the bipod down and dropped into a sitting position. It only took a second to ask Jimmy, "That's the one, isn't it?"

"Yeah!" he replied.

I stroked the trigger.

To my horror the buck was still up and running hard, almost immediately bouncing out of sight. We took off on a dead run. As we cleared the ridge, we stopped dead in our tracks. I was shocked to see a much bigger buck standing in a dip not 50 yards away. He had been hidden from our vantage point when I shot, and we hadn't realized that the two bucks had switched places. However, I had pulled the trigger and the die was cast. Only a few moments later we spotted the buck I hit struggling up a bluff. In short order, it was over.

Unfortunately, it was obvious the antlers were not as large as I first thought. It's not that the rack was small, just that it was smaller than many other bucks we had passed. Even the nontypical we passed earlier that morning would have scored higher. I was disappointed for a while, but then it sank in that I had shot the mule deer for my "triple-double" in the last half-hour of my last hunt. I was pretty lucky, at that!

In total, I had spent 13 wonderful days hunting my favorite quarry—big mule deer bucks. Along the way I had passed on well over three dozen bucks that would have scored at least 175 points while looking for a real monster. I had decided early in the game that I would go for broke, and if I had the decision to make again today, I would make it the same way. There are a lot of pluses wedged into my memory about this island hunt: the challenge and beauty of the ocean-side topography, the many "almost" bucks that I had passed, my new friends and time spent hunting with old friends, and even the emotional roller coaster of wounding "my buck."

That's the strength of hunting on Santa Rosa Island. It's a place where unique hunting memories are made in beautiful country rich with heritage, unusual hunting challenges, and the chance to tag a monster mule deer. It's the promise that makes Santa Rosa magic!

Buster
Bucks in
Utah

$\int$ EVERAL HOURS before sunup, the "call of nature" was so demanding and unrelenting that I just had to answer. I really hated to leave the cozy warmth of my sleeping bag for the cold and darkness outside. As I crawled out of the tent, an icy slap of wind hit me in the face and a mound of snow broke loose from the tent flap, cascading down my neck. I was instantly chilled to the bone and ecstatic. I had prayed that this would happen—the snow that is!

For most of the week we had tried unsuccessfully to find a big muley buck despite unseasonably hot temperatures and bluebird weather. Now we were finally getting the weather that I had hoped for when I booked the hunt many months earlier. Unfortunately, the year's first snow was falling on the last day of October; the last day of deer season, and more importantly, my last chance to kill a big Utah mule deer.

I jumped back into the warmth of the sleeping bag and for the next three hours listened as the wind and snow hammered the tent so hard that sleep was impossible. I passed the time reflecting on the last few days and an encounter with a buck that had occurred three days earlier. I was haunted by that stalk and nagged by the question that maybe we could have done something differently.

Gary Walker, my guide, and I had spent several days glassing from a ridge we nicknamed "the cedar knob." It was a great lookout for glassing up one of the huge bucks I hoped to find. The knob overlooked several canyons radiating to the north and flanked a sage-brush flat where we had spotted numerous bucks. Unfortunately, none of these bucks matched the bucks killed earlier on the ranch, including one monster scoring over 208 points. After my disappointment on Santa Rosa Island, I was even more determined to hold out for a buster buck and made Gary swear to smack me if I looked twice at any of the 180-type bucks that we frequently spotted.

For several hours we had picked apart nearby hiding places with our binoculars and had just switched to our spotting scopes to look into the farthest corners of the flat, a mile or more away. Way out there, one tiny spot just didn't look right. The horizontal shape was the right color, but out of place and much too big for a deer. Finally, the shape shifted and I could see that it was actually two does bedded, one slightly behind the other, facing in opposite directions and partially screened by the sagebrush. While I watched the does, off to the side a buck struggled up and started feeding, followed by several more does that I hadn't spotted. Occasionally, I would catch a glimpse of another buck hanging back in the brush. When that buck finally stepped into the open, I was astounded. I stopped breathing, fine-tuned the focus, took one look at the rack, and knew that I had found something special!

"There's a good one, Gary," I said excitedly, pointing in the general direction of the herd. I was excited both by the size of the antlers and because it was one of the few times that I had seen a buck before my guide. Gary found the buck in his scope and softly began to describe his trophy potential. "Great back forks," he said, "but I think he's only 26 or 27 inches wide."

My next question seemed bizarre. "Does he still have velvet?" Normally, by October the velvet is long stripped away. Still, we had seen another buck in velvet, so not only was it possible, but it could be an explanation for the exceptional mass of this buck's antlers. After a few moments of jawing back and forth, we agreed that we were not only looking at a trophy, but possibly a stag. We carefully evaluated each tine, and only after agreeing did we add our guess to the rapidly accumulating score. In the end, we thought that the buck would conservatively score between 190 and 195 points. Velvet would be icing on the cake!

We needed a closer look, but daylight was fading rapidly. We had less than an hour to cover a lot of ground. We took a last look to verify our count of five does and two bucks and hastily plotted a battle plan. Gary suggested that we run back to the Jeep, drive three miles down the canyon to circle the herd, and then hike up the backside of the bluff they were feeding toward. Easy for him to say! I had 20 years on him and more than a few pounds, but I was game. Besides, his plan seemed like the only way to beat the wind that would surely betray us if we tried to go right at them. I

Gary Walker takes a break during the heat of the day to teach us the fine art of throwing "shoes."

threw my gear in my pack, strapped it on, and started running downhill toward the Jeep.

The bouncing Jeep ride down the canyon was exciting, and I'm sure we missed some of the holes in the gravel road, but not many. Our white-knuckled jaunt cut a large circle around the herd to the back of their ridge. Gary jammed on the brakes, the Jeep plowed to a stop, and we hit the hill running, scrambling toward the ridge line. Gary, an old hand at stalking big bucks, seemed surprisingly calm. Not me. My throat was dry as paper, my heart was pounding, and my mind was racing through my pre-shot routine. We broke the ridge and started crawling through a screen of sage-brush, occasionally risking a peek over the cover to check the terrain ahead. We had already passed our landmark—the seventh telephone pole on the ridge. I was getting nervous because it was quickly getting too dark to shoot, especially because of the poor light-gathering ability of my long-range scope. If we could find the buck in the next few minutes, I still had a good chance to make the shot.

Gary stopped suddenly and trained his binoculars on a small ravine to our right. I froze in place. Could the bucks have gotten behind us as we were flying down the canyon? He finally relaxed, turned, and mouthed the word, "coyote!"

Slowly, we moved ahead, cautiously and quietly, glassing frequently. Only a glimmer of daylight still glowed in the sky. Where were they? The tension was broken with Gary's whisper, "There's the smaller one!" The next few minutes flew by as we frantically searched for the big velvet buck, but there was simply no sign of him or the does. Several times I raised my rifle to check the crosshairs, and then finally, dejectedly, poked Gary on the shoulder and shook my head. It was just too dark. Reluctantly, we backed out. We may have been only minutes away from finding the buck, but any shot in the dwindling twilight would be risky, and there was also a chance we could spook him clean out of the country.

For the next two days we hunted that area hard and never again saw the velvet buck. Now, with the falling snow came rising hopes. I lay in my sleeping bag, listening to the wind rattle the tent, recalling the sweat, sore muscles, and our fruitless warm-weather efforts to find the velvet buck. We had thoroughly combed the open country and invested hours painstakingly glassing every nook, cranny, and bush on the flat. The terrain was deceptive. What appeared to be gently rolling country with marginal cover was actually laced with numerous small cuts, depressions, and deceptively high brush that could hide Shaq as well as completely screen a herd of mule deer. I recalled several plainly visible bucks that simply disappeared as I watched, swallowed by the cover.

Still, the big buck had to be there somewhere. The ranch boundary was less than a mile west of where we had first found the velvet buck, and it would need to cross several canyons to get there. It was possible the buck had left, but not likely, since I didn't think that we had spooked him. With only one day left in the season, time was getting precious. Strangely, I was still optimistic.

As the wind howled and the snow fell, I was anxious to get out of my bag and into my hunting boots. This day had been a long time coming. This hunt had actually started almost two decades earlier when I had tracked down Kim Bonnett because I heard that he had killed some whopper bucks. The cadre of really dedicated mule deer hunters is a very small, close-knit community, and a hunter's success is soon widely known by those of us that keep up with those sorts of things. The rumors about Kim were correct. A trip through his trophy room is intimidating to those of us "wannabes" who have had marginal success taking the real trophy bucks.

I wasn't surprised when Kim and his business partner, Jeff Warren, built Bucks & Bulls Guides & Outfitters into one of the most respected hunting outfits for trophy antelope, elk, and, of course, huge mule deer. No hunting outfit is better than its guides, and Bucks & Bulls uses some of the best in the business. Several of the guides were also longtime friends of mine, the kind of guys we call deer nuts. Although I had written about the Bucks & Bulls operation a number of times, I had never shared a camp with them. The hunt was on my "to do" list after I retired, but I

Denny Austad holds his velvet-covered, 194-point buck taken during the early September hunt. This beautiful buck has a few small kickers, but otherwise it's the picture-perfect typical mule deer.

knew that I couldn't delay much longer because the day was fast approaching when I wouldn't be able to climb mountains and hunt hard. So my call to Kim for my triple-double project was predictable.

I pulled into camp for the last hunt of the season only hoping to match the success of Kim's early September hunt on this ranch, when his hunters had killed six bucks averaging an amazing 191 points. On our first night in camp, Denny Austad showed me the rack that he had collected on his September hunt. It had a 31-inch spread, and the velvet-covered six-pointer gross-scored 194 points. It was also the third big buck Denny had tagged while hunting with Kim and Jeff. Now Denny was back in camp to help his son, Brian Austad, and nephew, Scott Austad, on their management deer hunts.

Part of the reason Bucks & Bulls have been so successful specializing in big bucks is because the ranches they hunt are in Utah. The

Utah Department of Natural Resources supports private wildlife management with landowner incentives. The beehive state's Cooperative Wildlife Management Unit (CWMU) program is designed to allow ranchers who properly manage wildlife to benefit from their efforts. The state grants participating landowners preferred hunting seasons and guaranteed licenses in exchange for implementing state-approved wildlife management plans.

The CWMU also gives deer hunters the opportunity to buy landowner tags, bypassing the uncertainty of participating in very competitive state drawings. CWMU private land hunters also enjoy the advantages of hunting areas with strict harvest limitations and minimal hunter pressure, both necessary if an area is to produce topflight trophies consistently. The results are obvious. CWMU ranches annually lead the state in trophy production, and their deer normally outshine deer taken on adjoining public lands. Let me stress—they rely on improved habitat and sound management results to hold trophy deer and not high fences. The deer are free to leave the ranch.

My wait for the coming light while I lay there in my sleeping bag listening to the raging storm gave me plenty of time to relive the many other bucks that I had passed on during the last five days. One buck the first evening was an example of how our luck was to run. That day we had glassed at least two dozen bucks, so we were seeing plenty of game. None, however, had the potential of the one Gary saw walk out of a brush line just before dark. The buck was feeding two ridges east of where we were hunched behind our glasses, too far away to stalk before nightfall.

It wasn't that the buck was wide, because I doubt that his rack spanned 28 inches. Nor was he very heavy; but you certainly couldn't call him willowy. His back forks, however, were to die for. I'm sure that the G-2s were over 18-inches long, and the G-3s were at least 13 inches. Imagine, at least 62 inches of score in those tines alone! And, the one G-4 that we could see was also over 10 inches to boot. As the buck fed, we caught a few glimpses of the opposite G-4 and brow tines, but never long enough to form even an educated guess on how they would score. Meanwhile, it was getting darker, and as we watched, the buck simply walked back into the trees and disappeared. I turned to Gary and shrugged my shoulders. There was nothing we could have done but watch. We never saw the buck again!

If that buck had equal G-4s and even average brow tines, we guessed that he would have easily scored around 190 points, but as it happened, he was still walking around. Our major hunting problem had been the heat. Unseasonably hot days kept bucks bottled up until just before dark or bedding down shortly after sunup. The trick, which we had been unable to pull off, was to spot a trophy buck while there was still enough daylight left for a stalk.

On the fourth evening, management-deer hunter Bob Mays pulled into camp with the news that he had killed his buck, but had to leave it tagged on the mountain until morning. A native of Nevada, Bob was a seasoned hunter and had been trying to find an old buck with a rack long past prime. Bob's quest received a boost when Kim pulled into camp with the story of a buck he had spotted that morning that seemed to fit Bob's prescription. It was a wide, 4 x 4 with decent mass, but had weak back forks. Bob and his guide, Doug Peterson, started looking for the buck that afternoon. Eventually, they spotted a buck matching Kim's description, climbing a far slope. Bob found a rest, took a deep breath, and touched off. The buck hit the ground. The spread stretched the tape to 29-1/2 inches. There was some question if it was actually the same buck Kim had spotted. Either way, it was an older deer that was never going to develop the high-scoring rack Kim wants to kill on his trophy hunts.

Another hunter, Ken Trudell, sat on another memorable buck for most of the fifth day. Before lunch, he and his guide, Doug Spencer, had watched a big buck walk into a clump of cedars, presumably to bed down on a ridge isolated from the rest of the mountains. They saw him long enough to tell that the 4 x 4 would score at least 195 points, big enough to justify missing lunch. Ken and Doug carefully worked their way up to an outcropping where they could easily see the cedar tangle. They settled into their vantage point, prepared to spend the rest of the day waiting for the buck to get up that evening and begin to feed, when they would make the stalk and get the shot. However, after hours of glassing the thickets and wasting one of their few remaining afternoons, when darkness fell they were still waiting. The buck never showed. Apparently, it had continued through the obvious bedding area instead of bellying down for the day. Ken had spent a fruitless day staring at the brush, while the buck was likely far away asleep under some tree. It had dodged a bullet, unaware of how close he was to earning a spot on Ken's trophy wall.

Time crawls when you're pinned in a sleeping bag waiting for sunrise. By the time I heard the others stirring, I was already up, dressed, and hauling my gear to the Jeep. I was anxious to get going. The wind had finally dropped off to something less than hurricane force, and snow was filtering through the aspen canopy overhanging my tent. It would be a cold, damp day augmented by the first snow of the season. I couldn't wait. Because of the cold, the deer would be up feeding, but I was afraid the wind would give them an early push into the shelter of their bed. Kim's standing early-start policy of having hunters in position before first light—that magic hour—made even more sense today.

Everyone was grabbing a cold roll and cups of steaming coffee or whatever got them going in the morning just to tide them over until they returned to camp at midday. With the hunt on the line, Gary told me that we wouldn't be coming back for lunch. We were going back to the cedar knob, hoping for one last shot at the velvet buck. That was fine with me. My insides were churning with the prospects as we left camp.

The low overcast clouds and snow squalls fought back the coming light, giving us plenty of time to drive to the cedar ridge. Our velvet buck just had to be there somewhere, probably tucked out of the wind in one of those sagebrush-choked cuts. We had barely cleared camp when a small buck bounded across the road. Could it be a good omen? I was really stoked, looking forward to the day, but I have to admit that my restless, sleepless night began catching up to me when the warmth of the Jeep's heater soaked in.

Suddenly, Gary hit the breaks, shocking me out of my daydream, and pointed uphill to our left where I could see a buck and several does only 200 yards away. The buck was torn between the instinct for flight and the rage of the rut, but the does were simply milling around, keeping a wary eye on the vehicle at the base of the hill. The buck's quandary gave us time to carefully check out his rack. The only problem with this buck's trophy score was a narrow spread. The antlers were certainly heavy with a good frame that I pegged between 180 and 185 points. I was getting an itchy finger—thinking about that old bird-in-the-hand versus several-in-the bush proverb. I pulled my binoculars down and looked at Gary.

"Is he good enough?" I asked.

Gary looked me straight in the eye, and his words thundered in my mind. "Well, this is probably going to be the best day of hunting we'll have during the whole hunt!"

I relaxed and we continued driving, but not without some misgivings. Those hindsight second thoughts came back to gnaw at me while I was huddled under a ragged cedar tree glassing the sagebrush flat. It was colder than hell in the wind, which was whipping the snow, occasionally obscuring our view. I was chilled to the bone when we finally gave up and moved to the head of a deep canyon at the extreme edge of the ranch.

Gary didn't think that any of the other guides had ventured this far, and several of his September clients had killed good bucks in the canyon. Our walk to the overlook was pure murder; we ducked our heads and plunged into the throat of the wind, which was biting through even our heaviest coats. Worse, when we finally reached the edge, the only rack in the canyon belonged to a lone bull moose. By now, we were on Plan Z and were reduced to free-lancing it, prospecting blindly for a small area out of the wind where a buck might tuck away.

As it turned out, we weren't the only ones bucking the weather. We ran into Kim not far off the bottom in the ranch's last ravine.

He reported that shortly after daylight he had spotted another velvet-racked buck. This buck, he said, sported a 6- to 8-inch kicker tine. Kim had watched the buck bed, along with several other deer, not 100 yards from the fence. He assured us that the buck and his buddies were lying near a lone juniper on the hill, even though the sagebrush was too thick for us to see them.

Our plan was to backtrack down into the canyon, work our way uphill to where we could climb the ridge, and use the lone tree to screen us. Kim volunteered to hike around the north side of the ridge and walk the fence to spook the deer our way, if they should break in that direction. Gary and I slowly worked directly toward the unseen bucks. We hoped that the high sagebrush that had prevented us from spotting the bedded bucks would now prevent them from seeing approaching danger. We were carefully moving through the brush, making as little noise as possible.

I caught just a flicker in my peripheral vision. It was the velvet buck springing to its feet less than 40 yards away, followed immediately by four other bucks. In less than two seconds, all we could see were antlers bobbing through the brush and an occasional flash of their rumps to betray their direction. They were heading around the crown of the hill, probably to use it as a shield until they could turn and head toward the gully.

We ran full tilt downhill, hoping to beat them to the gully. The race ended in a quarter mile when we caught the herd crossing a small basin. Breathless, I dropped into a sitting position, found the velvet buck in the scope, and watched it climb the rise. I couldn't shoot. The buck was perfectly aligned with a smaller buck that I was certain also would have been hit when the bullet exited. I could only track him in my scope, waiting for my break, which never came. The buck disappeared as he and the other bucks lined out down the gully.

Moving again, we tried to keep the skyline at the top of the far ridge in sight. If they crossed, I might get a long shot. Despite hunting hard and moving fast for the next hour, we never saw the bucks again. Afterward, Kim tracked them far enough to see that

Don't be afraid to take a break from glassing. You'll be surprised how often you will spot a buck with your eyes.

they picked their way over the ridge, probably in the minute or so while we were crossing through the basin. There certainly was none of that mule deer stereotypical "standing-around-for-one-last-look" business, which many inexperienced mule deer hunters expect. This unpredictability is what keeps the challenge in the hunt and me coming back for big muleys year after year.

Later, after we all joined up again, I told Kim that I didn't want to chance killing two bucks, even if it meant my not killing a buck for my triple-double project. When we had first jumped these bucks, it was immediately evident that this velvet buck wasn't the one that we had chased for the last several days. Apparently, there were several bucks carrying velvet into November—most unusual.

Earlier in the week Scott had shot a 2 x 3 management buck, also in velvet that Gary and I spotted the second day. In camp later, Gary told me that it was a true stag—without testicles. Biologists I spoke with about this late-season velvet phenomena were unable to draw a single conclusion. One possibility, they said, is that the trait is genetic. There are also wild tales of cowboys roping fawns and castrating them in the spring. Whatever the explanation, Gary and I glassed up four bucks that still carried velvet during the last week in October. A buck like that would have added a novel exclamation point to my triple-double and a hunt that had now trickled down to the last few hours.

With no time to waste, Gary and I hustled to another canyon and took up stands while Kim and several of the other guides conducted a fruitless drive. Afterwards we headed farther up the canyon hoping to find a big buck Kim and Jeff spotted one evening only days before I arrived in camp. We climbed to the ridge line, dropped far enough over the top to make sure that we weren't silhouetted against the skyline, and once again started glassing. Deer were already up and feeding, including some smaller bucks that I didn't even consider in the half-hour of daylight left. I had resigned myself to going home empty-handed, when Gary whispered, "Lance, come here and take a look!"

Focused in Gary's spotting scope was one of the bucks that we came here to kill and probably the one Kim had found earlier. That buck certainly would have "booked," maybe even pushing the magic 200-point plateau! He was totally distracted, consumed with chasing a hot doe. All we could do was watch the show. He was over a half-mile away, and it was darned near dark. Between us and the deer there were two steep gullies and more tough terrain than we could negotiate in the time left. Still, it was fun watching a "shooter" while the last few minutes of light and my hunt drifted away.

Was I disappointed? Well, sure. But on the other hand, we had seen over a 100 bucks, including more than a half-dozen that would beat my goal of 180 points. I had decided to "go for broke," and as any gambler will tell you, broke is what often results. Besides, Gary would have gotten too much enjoyment out of smacking me if I had shot a smaller buck. One of the highlights was the two B&C candidates, and possibly a third one, that we spotted. How can anyone be disappointed with a hunt like that?

As the saying goes, "That's hunting!"

Pilgrimage to
El Carbon

T HE HOT MEXICAN SUN beat down on us only hours after it cleared the Sonoran sierra to the east. Our 4 x 4 truck was creaking and complaining as we dodged cactus, downed trees, and brush patches of thorn bush. We were crawling over deep erosion ruts in the soft desert floor, picking a path toward an area where rutting desert mule deer gathered. Guide Adan Celaya and I were struggling to hold on to our perches on the lurching truck and still scan ahead, hoping to catch a glimpse of hide in the shade or a tine shining above the cactus. At a distance, this cover had looked sparse, but in reality it was thick as hair on a dog, with one major difference—dog's hair doesn't poke, scratch, or stick you. Our big concern was losing an eye to the whips of mesquite branches or paloverde thorn.

Finally, we broke out of the tangled brush onto one of the many two-track roads on Rancho El Carbon. We had just turned south when Adan said, "Puma!" Rifle ready, my eyes darted through the brush searching under the trees for any sign of the cat. Chuckling, Adan pointed down. The track was clear and sharp in the sand where the lion had passed on his nightly jaunt, only hours earlier. We were not the only ones hunting this desert! The tracks continued for two miles down the road before the puma turned toward some low hills a short distance away where, presumably he was napping. The cat tracks were just one more reminder that we were hunting in an untamed land where surprises are the norm.

I was hunting on Rancho El Carbon one more time. After four hunting trips with my good friend, German Rivas, I know his ranch like the back of my hand. Still, it continues to provide surprises.

One minute I may be staring at seemingly endless patches of jumping cholla cactus, paloverde, ocotillo, ironwood, and mesquite, and an instant later I'm scrambling to kill a desert mule deer sporting a rack beyond the wildest imagination. Often, one of the diminutive white-tailed Coues deer erupts from the brush and streaks for distant cover. Surprises aren't limited to wildlife, and I'm pleased to find that I am fascinated with the desert. It's a land of harsh realities where water is in short supply and where animals and plants alike struggle for survival. Only the tough and resilient live. Yet, for all of its primitive harshness, the desert springs to vibrant life after one of the infrequent rain squalls. Birds perch high and sing loudly. Plants, which shortly before carried only sharp thorns and spikes of every description, soon display flowers and blossoms of every shape and color in the rainbow. It's a land that I have grown to love, and it has called me back to hunt at least once a year for more than a decade. My regret is that I should have started hunting in Mexico sooner.

Despite my love affair with Rancho El Carbon, my Deer Quest hunt there with my old friend German was largely a stroke of fate. In the spring, shortly after I conceived the quest, I had immediately called German, but with genuine sadness in his voice he had informed me that his hunts were already booked. We were both disappointed.

My second choice in hunting camps turned out to be a disaster when outfitter Ivan Flores left me high and dry at the last minute. Less than two weeks before I was scheduled to leave, I received a fax telling me that my scheduled trip had to be moved to a later date. He had booked some last-minute, high-dollar sheep hunts and wouldn't have guides available to meet his commitment for my deer hunt. He wanted to reschedule my hunt from the peak of the rut to dates that conflicted with my other scheduled hunts. It also meant that I would have to cancel my airline tickets to Hermosillo and change itineraries that had been set for months. It was a tremendous blow, not even considering the financial impact, and an impossible disruption to my very tight, multi-region hunting schedule. I was after my last buck in my Deer Quest, and even though I had another desert mule deer trip planned later in January, it was with an outfitter with whom I had never hunted. The prospect of throwing the dice for my final hunt with this outfitter, though he was highly recommended, on a ranch I had never hunted had me scared to death.

Then, Lady Luck smiled!

Only four days before my original flight was scheduled to depart, I received a late-evening call from Mexico. German's familiar voice informed me that he had just received a cancellation. It was music to my ears. It took him longer to tell me about the opening than it took for me to confirm that I was going. I already had my gun permit, travel visa, assorted paperwork, and airline tickets. It was a last-minute hunt, but there wasn't any last-minute scramble to make it happen. I would be in camp with only one other hunter, and I would again be hunting with Adan, who had guided me to the biggest desert mule deer I've ever killed. The holidays were suddenly a whole lot brighter!

The night after I arrived at the ranch, the other hunter, Andres Garza, was late for dinner, which is normally good news in a hunting camp, although we hadn't heard a shot. When the truck lights painted the hacienda's courtyard, we were all eagerly waiting. In the bed of the truck was a buck that most hunters can only dream of tagging. Just before dark, Andres and his guide, Ariel Oros, had spotted the buck traveling with a number of does. It took only a glance for Ariel to know that this buck needed to be shot, yet Andres was reluctant. He had never killed a mule deer and had nothing with which to compare it. He had no idea just how difficult it is to find a trophy buck like the one he was looking at standing under the mesquite 150 yards away. Complicating his indecision was the fact that it was the first day of his hunt, and he was thinking, "Heck, this isn't all that difficult, maybe I can find a bigger one!" Ariel was almost pleading with his client to shoot. The giant buck wasn't going to stand there for much longer. Finally, Andres succumbed and pulled the trigger. The first shot hit too far back, but the next one did the job.

It was a wise choice!

The 4 x 4 didn't break the magic 30-inch barrier, in fact it was only 28-inches wide, but it had everything else. My first impression was that it would score in the mid-180s, and I waited until after dinner to break out my tape. When it stretched along the main beam past the 25-inch mark, I knew immediately that I had underestimated the score. The proportions of the rack made it appear shorter and smaller than it actually measured. The final tally was 196-3/8 inches, netting slightly over 192 points. With bases over 5 inches, the tall rack, whose shortest major tine was 10-3/8 inches, was a trophy of a lifetime.

We celebrated Andres' buck long into the night, and the alarm's racket the next morning was not welcome. I had been hunting dawn-to-dusk for more than 80 days on my quest, and my tank was running on empty. It took noticeably longer each morning to work the kinks out of sore muscles. Thankfully, Andres' buck had rekindled my enthusiasm. Hunting is a sport where energy, patience, and optimism are necessities. However, my old tired body still didn't allow me to exactly leap into the back of the truck as first light was breaking, despite my mind coaxing, "Let's go!"

Within minutes after leaving the hacienda, we were hunting. The miles slipped by in the cool refreshing air, though it was nippy enough to require a jacket and light gloves. We had just left a gravel road when I saw an area off to our right, about 50 yards in diameter, which looked like a tornado had swooped down. Brush was snapped off at the ground, cholla was uprooted, and a trampling of tracks suggested a terrible brawl. Deep parallel ruts in the sand betrayed that a titanic pushing match had taken place, where first one buck had the advantage and then the other. The image of two bucks with swollen necks and bad attitudes locked in combat fired my imagination. It was welcome evidence that bucks were nearby.

We were hunting this spot because it was just over the ridge from where Andres had killed his buck and because Ariel had spotted many does. The area is hilly and somewhat isolated from

Andres Garza cradles his first-ever mule deer buck. Hard to imagine ever killing a better buck than this one; it has everything most avid trophy hunters seek.

the rest of the ranch, and it was worth the detour to see if another big buck had moved in to claim the fallen buck's harem. In January the rut is raging, and the resident does draw roaming bucks to this area. In a land where the deer density is extremely low, any advantage is appreciated.

As our truck crawled through the brush, Adan suddenly pointed uphill. Not 50 feet away a doe was peering over the cactus at us, and another deer was feeding to her right. Adan immediately jerked the *"teléfono,"* a length of twine leading from the high seat above the cab to the arm of our driver, Carlos Mendez. It was his signal to halt! As we watched, more and more deer materialized. The herd was feeding and weaving in and out of the brush. We could see one small buck, but in mid-rut a collection of this many does had to have a "boss" buck around. When we found him, he was unaware that we were anywhere near. He was one of the "almost" bucks—almost tall enough and almost wide enough to make a top-scoring trophy. He did, however, have a 6- or 7-inch hanger off his main beam that caused me to think twice. After a few minutes of arguing with myself, I decided to keep hunting. It was only the second morning.

Trophies like the one Andres killed are what keep me coming back to Rancho El Carbon, and German is the reason that big deer roam this ranch. He is a successful businessman in Mexico City, with a commitment to making El Carbon one of the top desert mule deer ranches in Sonora. Owning and managing a ranch hundreds of miles from his home takes a great deal of work and effort. His motivation comes from being a very experienced, worldwide hunter with a personal dedication to wildlife and conservation.

German enjoys telling stories of when he was a young man hunting this ranch. He would park his truck along the road, get his horse out of the trailer, and head into the desert for a few days of hunting. Interestingly, in those days, there were some monster bucks, but the big deer were few and far between. There has been a healthy increase in the ranch's deer population recently, including the possibility of record-book bucks.

The ranch originally stretched from horizon to horizon, but was eventually divided by the Mexican government into 10 tracts. Some of the tracts were given to local villages and are now called *ejidos*. Others became working ranches, such as Rancho El Carbon. Unfortunately, but predictably, many of the tracts fell into disarray and were abused by a series of owners.

The improvement of Rancho El Carbon started in 1995 when German took the financial plunge and bought the ranch. It was one of the ranches made famous when news of huge desert mule deer began to leak out of Mexico two decades earlier. German committed himself to returning the 7,800-hectare ranch to its former "glory days" and has embarked on a long-term deer management program. His first order of business was to remove the cattle, although he allows a few head from an adjoining ranch to graze in exchange for hunting rights there. German then added thousands of hectares to his hunting territory when he leased two *ejidos* adjoining the southwest corner of El Carbon. He also made a number of improvements on the ranch, including building roads, fences, and a comfortable hacienda, as well as installing the first wildlife drinkers and feeders in the area.

Mule deer will travel many miles to good feed and water, and German's efforts will undoubtedly reduce the impacts of drought on his ranch, its wildlife, and the surrounding area. In addition, he has planted large swaths of buffle grass, which has proven to be very good deer forage.

These deer management programs are already producing results and are expected to pay dividends for years to come. On my second hunting trip to the ranch, I killed a buck scoring 206 points. A friend also took a buck that scored 195 points, despite most of a G2 tine broken off. I know of two other bucks that scored 200 and 212 points that were tagged in recent years. The possibility of killing a giant buck like these was why I was there on my Deer Quest. On each of my previous trips I saw quality bucks, if even for only a moment, but they never came easy.

We had certainly paid our dues so far on this trip. Shortly after Andres left with his trophy buck, we were joined by another experienced guide, Francisco Gagiola, nicknamed Pancho. A skilled desert hunter, Pancho was a welcome addition to our team. We had tried every trick in the book to locate a buck. We sat for hours on end glassing the valley floor, and trudged miles looking for the sharp edges of a big buck track cut deep into the granulated dirt. Occasionally, we would follow a track, only to confirm that it wasn't fresh or that it belonged to a small buck. Despite our best efforts, we came up empty. The bucks just weren't moving during daylight, and I blamed the bright moon. You could read a newspaper at midnight.

Some hunters claim the moon phase doesn't make a difference, but I'm not one of them. The few bucks we had spotted had all been seen on the fringes of daylight. Since the bucks weren't going to come to us, we had to go to them, and that meant covering a lot of ground in the hope of coming across a big, rut-blind buck on the prowl for does.

On my fourth night in camp, after a wonderful dinner, German informed me that his daughter was scheduled for surgery. He wasn't asking me to cut my hunt short, because I

Mexican cowboys find some outstanding desert mule deer racks. While not trophy hunters, they still know a big buck when they see it. The author is holding just one of these great racks.

knew that he was committed to stay the duration. Still, I quickly decided that the next day would be my last on this hunt. I wanted to make sure that German was free to be with his daughter, because I would have wanted to be there had the situation been reversed. I'll admit it did increase the pressure a bit, but I was still committed to shoot only a good buck or leave empty-handed.

At dawn the three of us were glassing the *ejido*, hoping to spot a buck moving at first light. This area had a reputation for big bucks and is one of my favorite places to hunt. Not only did I kill my 206-point buck there, but on earlier hunts several other record-book trophies had given me the slip.

Even though time was precious, I took a moment away from glassing to just soak in the scenery. The desert was alive as the first shafts of light broke through the wisps of clouds hanging over the sierra to the east. Where the hill met the desert floor, javelinas were bickering, and deep-throated, melodious calls tattled on a covey of quail not far away.

It is my favorite time of the morning. The day is fresh and so full of promise. It's that promise that makes hunters eternal optimists and one reason I felt that "today was the day." The hunch was odd, almost out of place, since I had just spent four days in vain looking for a good buck. Of the few bucks we had found so far, I doubt that the best would have scored much over 170 points. The great rack on the buck that Andres had brought into camp the first night at least gave me something to daydream over and keep my spirits up. Still, we spotted only two small bucks that morning.

It was midday when we approached rolling hills on the southern end of the *ejido*. It was so far from the hacienda that when we had hunted here the previous year, we had pitched a spike camp to eliminate drive time.

Suddenly, a deer broke from cover and was running down a coulee. It was a Coues deer with a small rack, but I was happy for the "wake-up call." It had been a long, dry spell. The hard days of hunting and short nights were beginning to take their toll. I was having trouble concentrating, and worse, I was running low on patience and optimism.

After a short tactical discussion with my guides, I decided that I wanted to spend my last evening hunting in the east hills near where Andres had found his buck. We had seen more does there than anywhere else on the ranch, and that's the key to drawing rutting bucks. We would have less than an hour of hunting left after driving across the ranch, but I still had that morning's flicker of optimism and was confident that the east hills held my best chance. Besides, if the last few days taught us anything, it was that we would see bucks only just before dark.

On the way, we had to drive through a stretch of ground where the cover was sparse and I rarely saw deer. The three of us were sitting back, taking it easy, and enjoying the ride. I was just staring off to my right, distracted by the anticipation of arriving at the rutting grounds, finding the does, and, I hoped, a heavy-racked buck. I should have known better than to relax!

Sixty yards out two does were suddenly in high gear and moving away through the undergrowth. Pancho started counting out loud, "*uno, dos, tres,*" but I couldn't find the deer in my Leica binoculars. I glanced at Pancho and was surprised to see that he was glassing a small wash to our left. Adan muttered, *"muy grande,"* and I started to become frantic. Where? Where? Suddenly, I found a buck moving away, but he was a long way from a *"muy grande."* There had to be another buck. I swung the glasses farther to the left, and suddenly he filled my lenses.

My amigos must have been wondering why I wasn't spraying lead while I took precious seconds to check the rack. He was crabbed off badly on his left side, but the rest of the tines looked decent. I couldn't gauge width. The does were moving away and starting to pick up steam, and the bucks were slipping through a patch of cholla and ocotillo less than 150 yards off and would soon be gone. Still, I couldn't get a good look at the antler spread. The bigger buck had already entered the thickest part of the cover and was about to disappear, when at the last moment he turned to look back at several deer coming up behind him. Now, I could see that his antlers were well past his ears. The buck wasn't going to stand there forever, even though the rut was a powerful ally. When you see a good buck, there is no question—your mind just screams shoot!

The rifle seemed to leap into my hands, and my thumb rode the Winchester's safety to the fire position. It was an automatic response born out of hundreds of hours on the practice range. Crosshairs were settled on the "sweet spot" when I applied the final ounces of pressure on the trigger.

Even before the shot registered in my mind, I knew that it was good hit. Inexplicably, though, my "dead buck" had swapped ends and was heading toward us as if nothing had happened. He was really moving, taking 20-foot bounds in stride; jumping cholla and plowing through low brush. I readied for a second shot when the buck disappeared behind a mesquite tree and didn't come out. We waited for several tense minutes. Finally, I could stand it no longer. We raced across the ground to the tree. He was folded up, apparently dying in stride. The big buck had covered 50 yards with the top of his heart gone.

As we admired the buck, it slowly began to register that not only had I killed the final buck in my Deer Quest, but I had waited until the last half-hour of the hunt to do it. I was quaking with emotions that had been building for six long months, and took a few minutes to just enjoy the moment. However, my celebration was short-lived; there was little daylight left and we had work to do.

We quickly snapped the obligatory pictures, dressed the buck, and headed back to the hacienda. We arrived just as the last light faded behind the hills. German hadn't heard the shot, even

Riding a horse is one successful technique for hunting desert mule deer. The action can be fast and furious when a buck is finally spotted.

though we were only a few miles below the ranch house, and was surprised when we pulled up with the buck. I relived the events of the day long afterward over a wonderful dinner of authentic Mexican food and steaks fit for a king. My last night in camp was spent with a good friend swapping hunting stories and the comfort of several bottles of excellent wine.

My desert mule deer was a better than average Mexican desert muley, but there are larger ones there. Considering that I was running out of time, I think that I was lucky to run across this buck, and it was everything I had any right to expect. The G3 was crabbed on the left side, and a tine had been snapped off the right beam leaving a base larger than a 50¢ piece. The missing tine was at least 8 inches long, according to one ranch hand that saw the buck earlier. It would have been considered a "trash" point, but I think that its stub adds character to my rack. The rack was heavy, carrying over 32 inches of mass. Long brow tines added to the score. The 4 x 4 rack spanned 31-1/4 inches with main beams well over 25 inches long. The gross score of almost 175 points was just under the 180 points that I had set as a mule deer goal before my quest started.

Hunters sometimes kill outstanding bucks with relative ease, but for most of us it is painstaking work and an adventure spanning many years and many trips. My four trips to German's ranch over the last seven years have generated memories of beautiful, untamed country, usually under a hot sun, with treasured seconds of total pandemonium. I've been rewarded with outstanding trophies, as well as the excited memories of missed opportunities. It's the siren's song of memories that keeps calling me back to Rancho El Carbon. The existence of the ranch and German's dedication to desert mule deer gives me hope that I will be able to accept the challenge of hunting a monster buck there for years to come.

Looking back, I realize how fitting it was that I completed my Deer Quest on this ranch.

Treasure
of San José

I T WAS A warm evening in the Sonoran Desert with scattered
clouds forming over the sierra east of us. The sky promised to
deliver another of the spectacular sunsets that I always look
forward to during my hunts in Mexico. Now, if dusk would just
deliver that high-scoring desert mule deer that I also looked forward
to finding…

Earlier in the afternoon we had moved camp to Rancho San José
after spending four fruitless days chasing desert mule deer on
Rancho Las Calabazas to the east. The move was welcomed, but still
it had cut a half-day out of my hunt, which was rapidly coming to an
end. After making the move, we still had the late afternoon left to
hunt, plenty of time according to outfitter Oscar René Molina for
us to drive to the ranch's south fence line and circle back to the
hacienda in time for dinner.

Movement caught my eye in a row of scrawny paloverde trees running the length of a shallow ravine. Two does were just getting up to
feed. I heard Alfredo Cansio, my Mexican guide, whisper, *"muy grande!"*
Almost in the same breath, Bernie Hammers, a Kentuckian and my
hunting partner for the last several days, confirmed that he also saw the
buck. Finally, I saw him standing just inside the fringes of the brush. A
second later he wheeled. I didn't get a good look, but what I did see gave
me the impression of a high rack.

The racket he made as he dove off into the ravine spooked the two
does and several others that we hadn't seen. From our low position we
couldn't see well enough should the buck turn out to be a shooter, let
alone get a shot. A hill on the opposite side of the arroyo offered a better vantage point, and we headed for it rapidly. From there we would
be able to look down into the cover and spot the buck again. It was my

bet that he wouldn't leave the does. We were soon glassing into the ravine, which spilled into a much larger wash flowing around the hill where we were perched. The buck had to be somewhere below us.

As I had come to expect, Alfredo was first to spot the buck. With his help, I finally made out the partially hidden buck standing as still as a statue in the shadows of a palo fierro tree. Only a portion of his rack and front quarters showed 400 yards away, but I couldn't see enough detail with 10-power binoculars. Shucking off my pack, I quickly assembled my spotting scope and tripod. Higher magnification confirmed that we were looking at a good 4 x 4, with good, tall back forks but short fronts. There was a difference of opinion about the width, with Alfredo guessing 27 inches. Bernie and I thought that it was at least 3 inches wider. At a distance of four football fields, the size of a buck's body and the width of its ears can easily account for the discrepancy in our estimates. I watched the buck for more than five minutes and several times held it in my rifle scope. Finally, I accepted Alfredo's advice and passed on the shot. Getting good advice is one of the reasons why I hire a guide, but later, after talking with Bernie, I had some misgivings. Still, the 4 x 4 was the best buck that I had seen in four days of hard hunting.

This was the final adventure in my Deer Quest. It had started on Rancho Las Calabazas, a new ranch that Oscar had leased for the season. Earlier, while we waited for Bernie at the Hermosillo Airport, I had been encouraged by what Oscar told me about Las Calabazas and what he'd found on his scouting trips. By coincidence, while waiting at the airport, I ran into hunting friends who told me about four great bucks that they had seen on the ranch only two weeks earlier. One of them had missed several shots at a buck they estimated would have scored at least 200 points!

Our airport delay caused us to stay overnight in Hermosillo, and very early the next morning we drove north to the ranch. After impatiently enduring the delay and then being fired up by the story of my friend's 200-point buck, I didn't waste time getting into the field. Alfredo and I went to the south. Bernie went west with his guide, Raymond.

I have never hunted on any Mexican ranch where hunting conditions were better. The land had a balance of mixed trees and grass pastures, allowing good visibility with just enough dense brush to afford protective cover. Unlike my earlier Mexican hunt at Rancho El Carbon, here we would be hunting while cattle roamed the ranch. Most of the livestock was concentrated around the feed yards and water, and I hoped they would not complicate our deer hunt.

I felt better when, not long after leaving camp, we found a small herd of deer within one-half mile of a feed yard. A buck was standing behind a thin screen of brush, where he undoubtedly felt hidden. We carefully glassed him, and fortunately for him, I could see well enough to recognize that his fronts and G3s were too short for a high score.

By evening it had become evident that the range cattle would indeed be a problem. According to Alfredo, the rancher had moved the cattle onto this ranch only days before we arrived, and the stock was now spreading across the ranch. I also noticed that the deer we spotted in the afternoon didn't stand around for long. Bucks and does alike were extremely spooky and often ran for cover long before we were within shooting range.

That first afternoon Bernie pulled into camp with his buck, a 4 x 4 with a 23-inch spread. He seemed a bit disappointed and explained that before settling for his buck, he had bumped a 30-inch monster that got away. Bernie's problems started when he arrived at the Hermosillo Airport, but his baggage didn't. Oscar loaned Bernie a rifle to use until his missing baggage and his own rifle caught up with him. I could sympathize with Bernie's plight. It's tough shooting with a strange rifle, and it was that unfamiliarity that created a critical split-second hesitation when the "chips were down." Bernie pulled up on the 30-inch buck, but couldn't find it in the scope before the deer ducked into cover. The unfortunate chain of circumstances cost him a trophy.

However, knowing that Bernie's big buck and the ones my friends had told me about were still out there was keeping my enthusiasm fired. For the next 2-1/2 days, we pounded the ground, poking into every corner of the ranch. Unfortunately, the farther we went and the more time passed, the more I became convinced that the big bucks had moved out, probably pushed onto neighboring ranches by the intruding cattle. We were certainly seeing fewer deer every day, until finally on the last morning, we didn't see a deer.

After Bernie shot his mule deer, he joined Alfredo and me. Bernie still had a tag for a Coues deer, and we agreed that if we ran across a good whitetail, he was going to take the shot. We saw several small Coues bucks, but by the fourth morning we still had no meat. I was relieved when Alfredo told me that after lunch we would break camp and move to Oscar's main ranch, Rancho San José.

Over the last dozen years, while hunting in Sonora, I had heard many stories about huge-racked bucks on the sprawling ranches within sight of Hermosillo. Rancho San José was one of these ranches. On clear nights from Oscar's hacienda, we could see the lights of Hermosillo, accented by a million brilliant stars. Some of the ranches near this major city have been shot out, but not San José. Oscar has carefully conserved and supported the ranch's desert mule

Bernie Hammers and the desert mule deer buck he killed on Rancho Calabazas.

deer by adding water sources, controlling predators, and planting forage. He limits the number of clients to only eight a season, as compared with some outfitters who book 30 or more hunters. I was thrilled when I was able to book a hunt with Oscar during my Deer Quest.

The ranch was his family's home, and the modern hacienda has hot water, electricity, and comfortable beds. It is also well maintained, unlike many other Mexican ranches these days that are deteriorating for lack of funds and attention. Oscar's main cook, Guadalupe Rendon, is a great chef who kept our belts tightened with an outstanding mix of authentic Mexican and American meals. Quality wines augmented the main dinner meals, and there was always a supply of *cerveza* and soft drinks in the cooler.

Oscar's decision to change hunting areas proved to be a good one. That first afternoon we were back into deer. This kind of flexible know-how is one of the advantages of dealing with an outfitter who owns the ranch. I've had a lot of experience with ranchers on both sides of the border. My family managed a number of stockyards in Colorado, and ranchers were our business. So when I write about how impressed I am with Oscar's ranch, you can believe that it's praise well deserved. He is committed to providing topflight deer hunts for his clients. Each year before hunting starts, Oscar conducts a cattle roundup and pens the livestock at the hacienda for the duration of the hunting season. This allows the deer, many of which concentrate on the ranch during the rut, to roam freely in peace.

Our swing around the southern end of San José that first evening was very encouraging. So much so, that I was a little disappointed the next morning when I learned that we were headed north. Light had just begun to show in the east when we pulled out of the courtyard. Within a quarter mile of the hacienda we saw the first buck. Barely enough "shooting light" revealed the detail of its small rack. We left it after watching for only a moment, because it was a long drive to the north end of the ranch. While we traveled, Alfredo told us about a buck that had been missed by a client less than a week earlier. His hunter had two chances at the buck. The first evening, he missed twice. The next morning, he missed three more shots. Alfredo told me, "He is probably 32-inches wide and might score as much as 200 points!" I dubbed the buck "Lucky!" He would command most of my attention during the remainder of my hunt.

There was plenty of light for shooting by the time we arrived in the northern foothills. We started the hunt hiking down a ridge that died at the desert floor well over a mile away. Although Lucky was seen in the hills to the east, Alfredo suspected that the spooked buck might be holed up in one of several protected pockets between us and the flats. There were plenty of tracks on the ridge, indicating that enough does were still in the area to hold his attention.

We moved slowly, taking plenty of time to carefully glass the gullies, pockets of brush, and cover choking the bottom of the ravine. I didn't want to bump the buck if, as Alfredo suspected, he was somewhere below us. We watched for big tracks that might be fresh enough to follow. If we were fortunate enough to find a fresh track, success would depend on Alfredo's considerable skill in deciphering nature's evidence—an imprint in the sand, broken or nipped brush or cactus, and other faint hints of the buck's passing. Except for a water tank at the base of the hills several miles away, the only water available in this part of the ranch was the rainwater collected in basins worn out of solid rock, called *tinajas* by the Mexicans. Most of the *tinajas*

The hacienda on Rancho Calabazas provided comfortable accommodations.

were shallow basins fouled by the birds, small animals, and insects that also depend on these water sources. Some hunters believe that desert mule deer rarely drink water, but extract ample moisture from forage, such as the ironwood tree pod, or prickly pear, barrel, and cholla cactuses.

During the first half-hour of hunting, the most interesting thing we found was a meteorite about 6 inches in diameter. An unusual find, but it didn't get our heart rate going like a good buck would. Ahead, the ridge split, creating a pocket covered with brush. Alfredo and I crept quietly toward the cover. Bernie lagged back a few yards to give us room.

Suddenly, we spotted several bucks and four does moving ahead of us, apparently unaware that we were nearby. Moving slowly, they gave us plenty of time to look each buck over. The best one was a three-pointer with a 27-inch spread. We had just started moving again when Bernie hissed and pointed left toward the bottom of the ravine.

It didn't take binoculars to spot the buck standing there, but I quickly raised my glasses for a better look anyway. His antlers were definitely big—extremely massive, with deep forks and long tines. I can't remember ever seeing another desert buck with a rack like this one. They were exceptionally dark colored, and the towering back tines curved inward, almost touching at the top. Unfortunately, it was a 4 x 3, missing a G4 on the left side.

The buck was milling around several does he was tending and didn't seem overly concerned that we were standing on the ridge. As long as the does held, he would stay close. Finally, the does, with the buck following, trotted toward a tangle of brush and trees in the ravine. Without regret or chambering a round, I watched them go. Shortly, the herd cleared the next hill, and we watched them running for well over a mile before they disappeared into an arroyo chiseled across the desert floor.

Maybe I had made a big mistake by not shooting that buck, but Lucky was looming in the back of my mind. After the 4 x 3 left, we took a break, and only then did Bernie say that he thought that he had seen a stub where the missing G4 should have been. I hadn't seen any evidence of the missing point, but on several occasions during the hunt Bernie had demonstrated that he had outstanding eyes. There is a chance that I missed the stub. I'll never know, because we never saw the buck again.

After dinner that night we scored some of the sheds hanging on the fence surrounding the hacienda. One wrist-thick antler was particularly interesting, showing ample evidence of the quality bucks available. It was dropped by what we very conservatively estimated to be a 195- to 200-class buck. The shed scored a touch over 89 points, with its 18-inch G-2 point. While I was admiring the shed, Bernie ventured that in his opinion the buck we had let walk was maybe its equal, although much heavier! I don't think he was that big, but he was definitely a good buck.

Dawn was arriving in a cascade of crimson reflecting off the fleecy bottoms of scattered white clouds when we cleared the gate and headed back north in the crisp morning air. There were still several remote pockets that Alfredo wanted to check. It was my last day on San José, and I still had hopes of finding Lucky. The buck I killed earlier on Rancho El Carbon had relieved the pressure of filling the

After dinner on Rancho San José, the crew can be found enjoying a cool drink and warm fire.

desert mule deer slot in my Deer Quest. Now I was looking for a buck that would shatter my goal of 180 points.

The morning was spent poking around Alfredo's likely places, but by noon we still had nothing to show for our efforts. One small buck gave me a start when Alfredo whispered, *"Aya, el buro!"* When he said, "There, the deer," I turned to see that he was pointing behind us to a ridge almost devoid of cover. Standing under a lone paloverde was a buck, and I was amazed to see a doe there as well. Somehow we had missed seeing them. At first glance, I was impressed with the width of the buck's rack, which was close to 30 inches, but that was about the only good thing you could say about it. The rack's 20-inch main beams were the shortest I've ever seen on a buck with that kind of spread, and it was crowned with only three short tines to a side. It was an easy decision to keep going.

The sun that rose so spectacularly in the coolness of the fading night was now beating down mercilessly. Already the temperature had soared into the 80s, and mirages danced on the desert floor. The day promised to be even hotter by late afternoon. We had turned south toward the hacienda for a late lunch. The lunch and the siesta that followed was certainly worth the extra miles and effort. I was looking forward to the siesta today. My body was beat after more than 90 days in the field. At night I could no longer get enough sleep, and my energy didn't bounce back as it did in August. The thought of the *cerveza* cooling on the front porch tormented me as we cleared the hills and headed home.

As we neared one of the ranch's water tanks, I saw several white butts and the telltale black-tipped tails moving in the mesquites and creosote brush. One buck was nosing a doe ahead. He was a good one, with a tall rack that stretched far above its big ears. Raising my binoculars, I was quickly going through my checklist. Yes, he is high. Uh-huh, I can see four points on the side nearest us. Yup, the beams are thick. Getting a good look at the far side was difficult because the buck was busy rounding up his harem. Finally, I caught a glimpse of a very long G-4 on the off side; and at the same moment Alfredo said, *"cuatro,"* which I took to mean a 4 x 4. That's all I needed.

Foliage in the Mexican desert can be hostile to the careless hunter.

The shot was more like one you would expect while shooting sporting clays. I can't even remember the sight picture, yet I knew that with all of my off-season practice, when the crosshairs were lined up on the spot, the buck was going down. I squeezed. The buck flinched and spun around, obviously hit hard. His head was down and he was staggering. I whacked him again since I didn't want him to suffer one more second.

Walking up to the fallen buck was a revelation. What I thought was a foot-long G4 was actually an 8-inch, nontypical point coming off low from a back tine. The buck was really a 3 x 3 with eye guards and two nontypical points. On the positive side, it was certainly massive and tall. The longest G2 stretched over 20 inches. Another surprise was that, once again, I had clobbered a buck with a point broken off, this time it was a tine with a base that was almost 2 inches across. The point had probably been broken off during the rutting battles, and it hurt the rack's final score of 179 points.

My buck was one of those deceptive desert muleys that look a great deal better than they actually score. Still, it was also the highest-scoring desert mule deer in my Deer Quest. Complaints aside, given the same circumstances, I would make the same decision. When I shot, only a few hours were left on my last hunt of the year!

When I grabbed the deer to hold it for field dressing, the buck provided me with a painful payback and a reminder of lessons forgotten. The buck's legs and lower body were riddled with cactus spines and thorns. We needed gloves to hold the legs without getting speared. It's common to see deer in Mexico with cholla bulbs stuck to their faces and bodies. Anyone who has clashed with this cactus knows the pain involved. Yet, my buck was in excellent shape, and its rump was padded with an inch of white fat. These are tough animals that live in a harsh climate, with summer temperatures sometimes soaring above 115 degrees.

I wish now that we had hunted Rancho San José for the full duration of the hunt. Perhaps we could have found Lucky or the dark-horned buck again. I'm looking forward to hunting this ranch in the future. That night after a gourmet meal, Oscar told me that he would lease hunting rights on Rancho Las Calabazas again only if the rancher agreed to delay rounding up and moving his cattle. From what I saw, that ranch could be a great desert mule deer ranch, since it has not had an army of hunters on it over the last few decades.

My Deer Quest failed to produce one of Mexico's proverbial "monster mulies," those legendary bucks that can easily exceed a breathtaking 35 inches, but I tagged two desert mule deer bucks that were well above average. I also left Mexico with memories of big bucks that got away, which will give me enough to dream about while I'm sitting at the shooting bench waiting for the barrel to cool or shopping with my wife.

No doubt, there are big bucks still available south of the border. Some very fine bucks were killed there in 2001, including one that grossed over 220 B&C points. Several others stretched the tape to more than 38 inches. The prospects of finding one of these magnum bucks continue to draw me like a magnet back to the treasure of San José.

The author's high-racked desert mule deer buck has two nontypical points, as well as an assumed huge brow tine that was broken on its left antler. A quality buck to be sure, but other, bigger bucks were seen during the hunt.

Mixed aspen, oak brush and conifers provide perfect cover for big mule deer bucks in Utah.

A large-antlered, nontypical mule deer like the monster Wayne Long is holding is a once-in-a-lifetime trophy. This fine buck was harvested by Frank Beltrame only days before the author's return hunt on Santa Rosa Island. Quality bucks are possible, but they don't come easy.

Six mule deer bucks of this caliber killed during a three-day hunt on Santa Rosa Island is truly an incredible feat. Clockwise from top left: Jerry Wilkinson, Rod Fogle, Gary Amaral, Bob George, Greg Amaral, and Anne Chisum.

Gordy Long may appear to be watching one of the many whales present offshore, but he's actually glassing for a big buck spotted earlier.

Although not your typical mule deer habitat, the bluffs along Santa Rosa's beach are still steep and rugged.

Bob George shows the result of his single-shot kill on Santa Rosa Island.
Nontypicals like this one are trophies because they are so unique.

Bob Mayes, holds his
Utah mule deer buck
after retrieving it
from the field.

Its tripod-back points
are just one plus on
this trophy.

Our home away from home nestled in
this grove of aspen trees in Utah
included individual sleeping tents.

In addition, separate cooking and dining
tents made this a comfortable camp.

Long shadows accent the rack of the author's desert mule deer buck killed on Rancho El Carbon. The crabbed back tine caused hesitation, but the 31-inch plus rack still qualifies it as a good 'un.

Dense desert habitat makes spotting and killing a desert mule deer a challenge, especially while evaluating the rack in the few seconds before the buck leaves. A careless hunter also risks an eye when charging through this dangerous cover.

Hard to sneak up on and even harder to get a good look at when you arrive, this desert mule deer buck is just about ready to explode from cover.

Whitetail
Deer

The
King

T HE WHITETAIL is the mother of our deer species. First appearing over 4 million years ago, the species survived in the gaps between the ice ages when hundreds of other species were eliminated. Today they are the most populous and widely distributed big game animal in North America and some claim the world. We now hunt whitetails from Canada almost to the equator and from Maine to Washington. Incredibly, less than 100 years ago the entire North American population was estimated at less than 500,000 animals.

While an individual whitetail's home range can be measured in only a few acres, the range of the species is huge. It covers an area from northern Canada, every state in the lower 48, most of Mexico (except Baja California), all of Central America, and the northern part of South America. Within this immense range are several subspecies of whitetails, including the popular Coues deer. There are also regional variations in body sizes, as well as marked differences in the ears, tails, and seasonal body pelage.

In their northern range, whitetails are generally large bodied, with small ears, short tails, and dark coats compared with subspecies at the southern end of the range that are usually light colored and small framed, with large ears and wide tails. These variations in body confirmation are nature's solutions to regional temperature variations—cooling in the south and heat retention in the north.

With so many variations of whitetails spread across such a huge area and often overlapping ranges, wildlife managers and scientists have had difficulty identifying and describing individual subspecies. Opinions vary from expert to expert. One noted scientist, Mr. Whitehead, lists 38 subspecies, including eight from Central and

South America. His descriptions were based on scientific data, without consideration for the difficulties of establishing and administering record books, not to mention confusing hunters.

Safari Club International's (SCI's) record book system includes seven whitetail categories: northwestern white-tailed deer, northeastern white-tailed deer, southeastern white-tailed deer, Texas white-tailed deer, Coues white-tailed deer, Mexican white-tailed deer, and finally Central American white-tailed deer. North America's other major record-keeping organization, Boone and Crockett (B&C), has established two: Whitetail and the Coues Whitetail. The B&C system seems the simplest since the Coues whitetails are not known to touch the other whitetail ranges. I used their logic to organize this book.

Whitetail

So much has been written about the white-tailed deer that it is impossible here to add much more, other than my personal experiences gained from more than 30 years of hunting them. I've been lucky to chase whitetails over much of their range, from Oregon to Virginia and from British Columbia to Mexico. Still, I've barely touched hunting whitetails in all the nooks and crannies where they live and under all of the hunting conditions where they are found. So my comments will have to be taken in that context. I don't pretend to know "all" about whitetails; heck, I won't even pose as an expert. There are, however, a few things that I have learned that may be of value.

In the mule deer section of this book, I alluded to the breeding advantage that whitetails hold over mule deer and why they are slowly, but certainly, encroaching on historical mule deer ranges. I have seen this first hand in my home state of Oregon. Thirty years ago whitetails were only rarely spotted in the northeast corner's Snake River–Hells Canyon drainages. West of the Cascades, Oregon had an isolated and scattered population of whitetails. Today, the northeast region supports a healthy, growing population. I believe they drifted into Oregon from Washington, south through the Columbia River system, and from Idaho, west across the Snake River. In Oregon and much of the far West, this expansion has been a recent phenomenon that is accelerating. I was present when the first Oregon B&C book buck was measured at a sportsman's convention less than 15 years ago. Since then more whitetail entries have been recorded from this state. The other western states and provinces are experiencing a similar extension of whitetail range propelled by exploding populations.

Most hunters in the southern and eastern United States have also witnessed a dramatic increase in whitetails, so much so that today in some states the seasons and bag limits are quite liberal. As another example, I am told that decades ago whitetail sightings by residents in the Midwest were rare. Today, many of the states are widely known for healthy herds and trophy-quality bucks.

Whitetails are fascinating to hunt, a statement with which most hunters would agree. According to many writers, however, they are the craftiest animal in North America and the greatest hunting challenge. Because of this media blitz, most sportsmen are convinced that whitetail have nearly supernatural instincts that make them almost impossible to hunt and kill. This is especially true for bigger bucks. I'll grant that any whitetail is a challenge and a big buck rarely comes easily, but while I respect them, I believe that the aura of the whitetail has been greatly exaggerated.

Perhaps I've been lucky. Certainly, I've tried to hunt in places with big bucks. I'll admit that I've never killed a buck qualifying for the B&C all-time recognition, but I'm certainly not alone in that claim. I have, however, killed several whitetail bucks that scored over 160 points. That said, I'll also divulge that the whitetail that I killed during my "triple-double" project missed my goal by more than any other deer species. Certainly, I had chances to shoot better bucks, but for one reason or another didn't, and the results surprised me. When I conceived my Deer Quest, I originally believed that both of the whitetail species offered my best chances to kill bucks that would be much larger than my goals. My premonition was accurate where Coues deer were concerned. Both of my Coues deer bucks beat my goal of 100 points. Not so with the whitetail bucks, but that's hunting, and perhaps next time the results will be reversed.

I feel compelled to offer a few comments about what I feel are widely held misconceptions about whitetails as a hunting challenge. My purpose is not to knock the whitetail, but rather to bring some reality and balance to the claims and emphasis given to whitetails. It seems that you can't pick up a magazine or watch an outdoor TV program without seeing a segment on whitetails, usually emphasizing the wariness of these bucks and the difficulty of dropping a trophy-class animal. Wary, yes they are, but they also have weaknesses that I feel can be exploited.

Take, for example, the fact that unlike mule deer, most whitetails are not migratory and live most of their lives in a very small area, sometimes less than a square mile. They can be patterned by hunters because they often use the same trails and bedding areas their entire lives. The now-popular patterning technique was, in fact, developed by whitetail hunters. Few other animals have received more attention and research regarding their habits, and the results are well known by knowledgeable hunters. Patterning is the ability to find a buck, determine its feeding and bedding areas, locate the travel paths between feed and bed, and set up an ambush point. Once patterned, most whitetail bucks can be killed by the patient hunter, given enough time. Even when the whitetails are primarily nocturnal, they will eventually make a mistake, especially in the rut when bucks are roaming far and wide hunting for receptive does. This is proven time and time again on the weekly TV programs, where hunters move into an area, construct a tree stand, and then wait. The trick is knowing how to find a big buck, figuring out its pattern, and then having enough time to execute (pun intended) the plan. In my mind, what sets whitetails apart from many other species is that hunter success requires a thorough knowledge of the species, the ability to figure out how to set up the ambush, and, finally, skills to kill the buck. Of course, in hunting many other deer species, patterning, setting stands, and such are not applicable.

Some years ago, while in Alberta, I had the chance to hunt what may have been a world-record whitetail buck. Gary Drinkall, an

Alberta outfitter at the time, and I were on a busman's holiday. Gary, several friends, and I trailered a jet boat from Washington state north to the Peace River on the border between British Columbia and Alberta. We wanted to hunt the Breaks of the Peace, which are famous for big whitetail and mule deer bucks. Our float hunt was planned during the last 10 days of Alberta's deer season. We expected to be on the river for 7 days, and leave 3 more days open after the float trip. If we found a stretch along the river that showed promise, we could stay and hunt; otherwise, we could power through the remaining stretch of river to the boat ramp and hunt elsewhere.

The late November weather was brutal, with morning temperatures pushing minus 30 degrees. One of our morning chores before we could continue traveling was to break chunks of ice off the boat, some over a foot thick. It was miserable in our mobile tent camp, and to make it worse, I didn't fire a shot. I was disappointed when we pulled out at the boat ramp, but little did I know that my adventure was just beginning!

When we landed at the take-out, Brian Cunningham, one of Gary's guides, was waiting with exciting news. While we had been floating and freezing, Brian had been scouting around Fairview for a place to hunt—just in case—and had located a magnum buck. He was able to watch the buck at close range for almost 15 minutes after it crossed a gravel road and fed along a power line. Brian has killed several whitetail bucks scoring 190 points or more, so his excitement was my first clue that he had found something special. He had seen the buck a second time only days before we arrived. The second look convinced him that it was an outstanding buck!

The afternoon we hauled out the boat, we stopped at a local sporting goods store where they were displaying a whitetail buck's rack brought in a few days earlier scoring 204 points. I held that rack while admiring its mass, tine length, and extreme spread. On our way out of the store, Brian whispered, "The one we are after is bigger!"

One problem is that we couldn't get permission to hunt on the farm where the buck was spending his days. Brian did, however, get the go-ahead to hunt several surrounding properties, including an important, wooded quarter section where the buck was frequently refreshing his scrape line. Only two days were left in the season when we started hunting him. The next day Brian and I agreed to "dog" for one of Gary's clients, since it was his last day. The client took a stand along the scrape line while we pushed some surrounding thickets. It was nonproductive, but we did confirm that the buck's main travel lane between his bedding area and several grain fields went through this quarter section. We had only one day left in the hunting season.

The next morning we were up before light and waiting on a stand located at the head of the buck's scrape line, as near to his bedding area as we could get. We had permission to hunt the two properties that stretched behind us to the south and hoped to intercept the buck that morning on his way back to his bedding area. By 10:00 a.m. I had lost faith in our hunt plan, when another buck broke out of the edge of trees chasing a doe south of us. I shot him. He scored more than 160 points, but still, I was disappointed. It may have been my only chance to hunt a potential world-record whitetail.

I believe that the time we spent hunting on the Peace was the reason we didn't kill that monster buck. One day, or even two days, is not enough time to kill a buck like that unless you are incredibly lucky. After all, Brian had seen him twice while we were on the river. The trail the buck had worn in the snow and his fresh scrapes showed me, without any doubt, that he was there—it's just that we weren't! Many big bucks are ambushed each year on patterned trails or over scrapes and from stands. Pattern hunting gives all hunters, especially archers, a prime opportunity to take a whitetail.

Another of the so-called truths that often appears in print is that the trophy whitetail is the most difficult quarry in North America. Some writers defend this opinion by comparing the total population of whitetails with the huge number of hunters in the field and the paltry number of B&C entries. Their explanation disregards the fact that an increasing amount of the whitetail hunting is taking place on game ranches, which, of course, are not recognized by B&C.

For example, Texas has a high whitetail population, but many of the really big bucks are grown and taken on private ranches enclosed by deer-proof high fences. The truth is that many outstanding bucks featured on the televised hunting programs are killed behind fences. This is not an indictment of hunting behind fences, because I think that such preferences are best left up to the individual. Ranched whitetails are, however, a fact of the whitetail hunting scene today and complicate accurate record keeping.

I've already given my opinion about the difficulty of hunting other deer species. If you still believe that the whitetail is the most difficult animal in North America to hunt, then I will offer one more candidate to consider.

What about the difficulty of killing a cougar without dogs? I've spent most of my life in the outdoors, often in country with high resident populations of mountain lions, and sat for thousands of hours behind binoculars. Yet, I've seen fewer than a half-dozen lions, and most of those have been seen in the last few years in Mexico. I suspect that the challenge of killing a cougar without dogs is the most difficult hunting challenge in North America, if not the world. By comparison, it's common to see many whitetails in a day. I'll concede that we won't see free-range trophy bucks daily, but in many places in Canada and the Midwest it's not uncommon to see at least one big buck on a hunt.

Disagreements aside, whitetails are certainly a worthy quarry and one enjoyed by hundreds of thousands of hunters each fall. I've enjoyed every hunt I've ever had pursuing them.

One of my most enjoyable hunts was a whitetail hunt in Virginia. I was working in Washington, D.C., at the time, and a co-worker had a little cabin where the men in the family congregated every fall for their bonding ritual. To be a part of that experience was something special. I didn't get my buck, but it was the first time I watched deer legs under short pine trees—trees so thick I couldn't get a shot. To a young man born in Colorado and accustomed to hunting the wide-open prairie, whitetail brush hunting was a revelation.

Since then I've hunted whitetails using a wide variety of techniques, including drives, ground and tree stands, still hunting, and rattling. All have paid off for me, but if there is one lesson that whitetail hunting teaches, it's that no method will be successful all of the time. I've never hunted with dogs, as they do in the South, but having seen the swampy country where they hunt, I can understand why it is popular. I have little doubt, however, that the most successful technique for killing a trophy whitetail is to let him come to you.

The subject of where to hunt a big whitetail is covered in many articles, ad nauseam. Entries have been recorded in record books from every province and state within the whitetail's range. This diversified balance of potential trophy range is a big plus for whitetail hunters. Even hunters who never venture outside of their home states have a chance to bag an outstanding trophy. There are whitetail hot spots, of course, and they vary over the years. In recent years, the Midwest states and provinces of Alberta and Saskatchewan have produced more than their share of big bucks. Years ago, many authorities thought that the next world record might come from Idaho, of all places.

The whitetail is truly the people's deer, and it is certainly the most adaptable deer species. We are lucky to have such a species— one that is abundant, challenging, and one of our most handsome trophies.

Coues Whitetail

This little whitetail deer was named for the naturalist, Dr. Elliott Coues. If you want to start an argument in a Coues deer camp, listen closely to how your hunting partners pronounce the name and then dare to use a different pronunciation.

The two most common pronunciations are "cows" and "cooz." I've been told that the good doctor pronounced his name "cows," so technically I suppose that would be proper. Yet, friends of mine, who by anyone's definition are Coues deer-hunting nuts, use "cooz."

However, another buddy of mine insists on using "cows"—I suspect to irritate those of us who prefer to use "cooz." Most Mexicans call these little whitetail, venado cola blanca.

No matter how you pronounce it, this little deer is, as the Irish would say, a "cracker." I truly enjoy hunting them, especially in Mexico, where many ranches offer a chance to kill a big buck. The weather is normally warm, and the quarry is a worthy adversary. I've hunted them in New Mexico, Arizona, and in two states in Mexico. I've killed 16 bucks, but still, I am a relative newcomer to hunting the "gray ghost" of the desert. I've had some great hunts, and I've been lucky.

I'll never forget my first Coues deer buck. It was in New Mexico, and one of the guys in camp was an experienced Coues deer hunter, having lived in Arizona for many years. On the first day, I brought in a buck that had fooled both my guide and me. Before I pulled the trigger, we had the rack scoring in the mid-90s. On the ground, it scored 88 points and change. The purpose of this story is that while the buck was smaller than I wanted, the experienced hunter was impressed because in all of his years of hunting them in Arizona, he had never killed a buck scoring over 90 points. Such is the challenge of this little southwestern deer. I believe that only a handful of hunters have the skills and dedication to consistently kill Coues deer bucks in the United States, let alone trophy bucks.

I have noticed that dedicated Coues deer hunters are fanatics, almost to the point of cultism. They live and breathe hunting these little bucks. Some of the diehards have become true "desert rats," a lofty distinction once reserved for wandering prospectors. I can see what draws these hunters. Coues country is beautiful in a rugged sort of way; the weather is comfortable, and the challenge of hunting these bucks is extreme.

Most new Coues deer hunters are surprised to learn that these deer are seldom found on the desert floors; rather, they most often inhabit the surrounding hills and mountains. I have hunted them at elevations up to 7,800 feet and in all of the habitat transition zones from pine trees to oaks and ocotillo to cholla. While most of the desert terrain in the Southwest is actually at deceivingly high elevations, more often than not hunters will need to look in the nearby rugged high country to find Coues deer. Generally, this means a tough hike beyond the reach of 4 x 4 vehicles, where sometimes even horses are challenged. The best hunting seems to be in the most isolated pockets.

The Coues deer has all the same inherent skills and natural abilities for evading hunters as its cousin whitetails, with one major additional advantage: they are small and extremely difficult to see. This requires specialized hunting because success often depends on sitting for hours on some mountainside glassing until the buck is spotted and then figuring out how to kill him. Typically, we use powerful optics, sometimes up to 30-power binoculars, anchored on good tripods, and scan every bush and rock crevice within a mile or more. An experienced Coues deer hunter will look for parts of a deer, not the whole animal, which is rarely visible. Refined glassing skill is what separates successful hunters from the rest. Even with quality optics, glassing is not easy. Coues deer are perfectly camouflaged by nature to blend into their habitat; I believe better than any of our other deer species. Once you spot a deer, don't take your eyes off it. I've located bedded deer, moved my glasses briefly, and then been unable to find it again even though the deer hadn't moved. Lots of trophy Coues escape for no better reason than either we just don't see them or we lose track of them during the stalk.

Finding a Coues buck is only the start of the challenge. You still have to figure out how to stalk close enough to kill him. They live in country that by other whitetail standards is wide open, and this further complicates stalking. Because these deer live and die in small areas, most bucks are so familiar with their surroundings that anything new or out of place immediately draws their attention. Try to imagine living your entire life in several hundred sparsely covered acres and think how well you would know every rock, bush, and crevice. And to make it even tougher, Coues deer can see as far as we can glass. It's ridiculously hard to sneak up on them.

Several of my friends, who are now enjoying remarkable success with Coues deer, began getting results only when they changed their style of hunting. They started using high-magnification binoculars mounted on tripods and practiced shooting at ranges most of us would call extreme. These guys are fanatical about their sport. They practice shooting at 500 yards until they're as comfortable throwing a bullet a third of a mile as the rest of us are with shooting 200-yard targets. Typically, they will also use a spotter, not unlike our military snipers. Specialization extends to their shooting technique. They prefer to shoot from prone positions, using a pack or bipod for a rest. They depend on 20-power scopes and big-caliber tack drivers. This combination allows them to shoot sub-minute of angle groups, and they do it with such consistency that they convinced me to adopt their techniques. Since that tactical breakthrough, I have taken four Coues deer bucks that beat the B&C awards minimum of 100 points, shooting out to ranges exceeding 500 yards. I'm still learning and practicing.

The majority of the big Coues racks entered into the record books are from Arizona. That statistic may now be somewhat misleading since hunting them in Mexico started in earnest only within the last decade. A large number of big bucks are coming out of Mexico, and some real wall hangers have been taken in Chihuahua and Sonora.

Those wall hangers are why I hunted in those Mexican states during my Deer Quest. I believe that the chances of taking an outstanding buck today are better south of the border than anywhere else in the Coues deer range.

Whitetails
in
The Black
Hills

IT WAS CHILLY even for Wyoming. Bitter cold burned our lungs and stung our cheeks as guide, Paul Burns, and I crawled out of his warm truck and started hiking. A steep grade dropped into a ravine and then turned sharply upward cresting out on a knife-like ridge more than a thousand feet above us. The ridge was scared by a rugged cut we called The Gap, our gateway to promising scrub oak and ponderosa pine thickets where we hoped to find a trophy whitetail buck bedded.

I was hunting on the Tope ranch at the north end of the Black Hills with my good friend Mike Watkins. Mike and his wife, Ester, own Trophies Plus Outfitters and offer hunts in three states: the southeast corner of Montana, the northwest corner of South Dakota, and Wyoming. Their comfortable lodge is located in remote Alzada, Montana, where, if you blink, you may drive past the bar, post office, and combination grocery store/gas station without noticing. That's fine with the Watkins because the numbers of whitetails, mule deer, and antelope more than make up for the lack of people, and there is almost no hunting pressure.

Other hunters in camp were after mule deer, but I was back looking for an outsized whitetail buck. Odds were good that I'd find one on 350,000 acres of neighboring ranch land Mike has leased. Most important to my hunt, Mike's hunting area included 22 miles of prime river-bottom whitetail habitat.

The year before I had hunted the west side of the ridge Paul and I were climbing by hiking through The Gap from Horse Pasture on the Tope ranch. The ridge formed a mini-divide with deep draws dropping away on both sides toward pastures several miles away. Paul's hunch that this spot should hold bucks had proved right. Deer trails were worn across the ice-covered slides in The Gap where deer traveled to feed in the pastures below. We had seen a few bucks streaking though the dense pines, but they were always gone before I could get a shot. At the end of my first hunt, we agreed that we needed a different strategy to hunt The Gap. Bumping deer in the cover and relying on blind luck wasn't working. If we could get to the top of the ridge, we would have a bird's eye view into the draws, meadows, and pockets below. From that vantage point, we might spot bucks lurking under the protection of the ridge and have enough time to check out possible shooters. All those pluses, though, were just hypothetical because we couldn't find a way to climb up there. A vertical cliff on the west side looked impassable, and we hadn't been able to spot another route.

The challenge must have bothered Paul all winter because, as soon as I arrived in camp for my Deer Quest hunt, he proudly announced that he had found a route to the top. I was his guinea pig.

Paul's route threaded through the cliffs, all right, but it was steep and slippery. Unfortunately, a storm was bearing down that promised to make the climb more difficult, if not dangerous. In late November, fallen leaves covered the steep hillside. Glazed with the wet snow that was filtering through the overhead branches, the leaves were now slick as ice, making our climb downright treacherous. Slowly, we worked upward, in places using tree limbs like ropes to help boost ourselves up to the next foothold. We slipped and struggled our way to the top, paused a minute to catch our breath, then eased out to the edge of the drop-off.

An icy blast of cold wind hit me in the face. During the climb, we had been protected behind the hill without a clue that we would soon be glassing down the throat of a 30-mph wind while being peppered with snow. We stuck it out for several hours, while chilled to the marrow of our bones. We saw deer and even a small buck, but nothing worth stalking. The intensity of the storm was increasing, visibility was decreasing, and finally we

One of the most consistent ways to kill a trophy whitetail in this country is to spot him first, then plan a stalk. Sitting for hours on end while glassing can be a bone-chilling experience, especially in the snow.

realized that we were wasting our time. Our trip off the hill was even more treacherous than the morning's climb. Several inches of white stuff had accumulated while we were on top, and the footing was even more uncertain. The strenuous descent was a serious test to see if my knee surgery only a few months earlier had really healed.

As nasty as the weather was getting, I was still thrilled! We were facing the first major storm of the season. Hunters who venture into these mountains, especially late in the season, know that changing weather is part of the game. Within a few hours, weather can change from calm, clear, and warm into a howling snowstorm that lasts for days. I was prepared for a storm and looked forward to it! Some of my best bucks have been killed under exactly the same conditions, especially after a prolonged storm finally broke.

Right now, though, a cup of hot coffee in the warm ranch house sounded mighty good before we headed to one of Paul's hot spots along the Belle Fourche River. We were within sight of Tope's ranch house when Paul slowed the truck, then stopped, and pointed toward Horse Pasture on our left. I could make out a dozen whitetails trying to get a few last bites before the worsening storm drove them into cover. A buck was standing on the fringes of the pasture, nearly a half mile away. Driven by the gusting wind, snow came at us in waves, partially obscuring the herd at times. The wind bounced my tripod-mounted spotting scope, but not enough to keep me from seeing the tall 4 x 4 antlers that we guessed would score nearly 150 points.

It was a good buck, but he wasn't the buck that interested me. Paul told me earlier that his running mate would score at least 10 points more. We hoped that the big 5 x 5 was either hidden in one of the folds that dimpled the field or tucked into the draws surrounding the pasture. The big buck had been seen in the pasture three days earlier, but not since. These Wyoming whitetails were in full rut and traveling far and wide looking for does. He might show up any time and any place.

We quickly abandoned any thoughts of coffee and were soon circling the field to where a small knob would allow us to sneak within 300 yards, sure killing range even in the howling wind. As I climbed the knob, I noticed small snowdrifts building in the long grass and made a mental note to remember to extend the bipod legs far enough for a sitting shot. Crawling over the top, I didn't need binoculars to see the does in the field. Several more deer were lying partially hidden in the surrounding trees. Raising my binoculars I confirmed that one of the bedded deer was a 3 x 2. The 5 x 5 was nowhere in sight. Paul nudged me and pointed to our right, where the 4 x 4 was slowly walking away into the brush. The rest of the day was a bust. The snow had driven the deer into heavy cover, and it was obvious that we had to get in there with them. That evening, over one of Ester's wonderful meals, we made plans for our next morning's hunt on the nearby U2 Ranch.

The U2 ranch was the backdrop for a series of Marlboro ads featuring cowboys, horses splashing through streams, and the most beautiful surroundings anyone could imagine. What made the ranch memorable for me, however, was the whitetail bucks Paul and I found there on our first hunt together.

The storm was still raging the next morning, and I prepared to be out all day. It was still dark when Paul left the kitchen table to start his truck. When he returned, he was grumbling that the gusting wind had already drifted the snow up to the bottom of the door panels. As he slipped off his Sorrels, he just shook his head, probably remembering the cold, wet, miserable day we spent together the prior year.

Grabbing the biggest insulated coffee cup I could find, I barked, "Quit whining. Let's go hunting!" Chuckling to myself, I turned and headed outside before he could reply. It isn't often that the ol' man would get one in on his young guide. I also knew that before the day was done, he would probably be hauling my sorry butt up some hill. Most other hunters would have looked at the storm, pulled up the covers, and gone back to sleep. Not Paul and I. We knew where to find deer, but suspected that the hunting wasn't going to be easy, nor fun!

The year before in a blinding blizzard on the U2 ranch, we had walked up a draw to the backside of an unnamed ridge. The protected slope was out of the wind, and deer were bedded there waiting out the storm. It was tough going, slipping in the snow and plowing through drifts that hid logs and branch tangles. The whitetail bucks were holding like quail; even when they saw us, they would often let us approach to within mere feet. When they did go, it was nothing but a shower of flying snow, rumps, whirling legs, and white flags waving good-bye. Our plan was to repeat what we learned the prior year with one variation: we would try rattling, as well.

It was snowing sideways when Paul turned off the gravel road. We locked in the front hubs and began clawing our way up a faint two track. When we cleared the top of the ridge, the wind dropped off as expected, and we parked. After sitting for several minutes to let things settle down, we slipped out of the cab and started down the road. Six inches of fresh, quiet snow gave us the best possible chance to surprise a bedded buck.

After a half-mile of walking, though, I was surprised that we had nothing to show for our efforts. Tracks revealed that a few deer were still moving, despite the blizzard, but probably at first light.

As we approached a small meadow, Paul pointed to his rattling sheds slung over his shoulder. We found a spot where our silhouettes were broken, tucked in, and tickling tines soon reverberated in the crisp, cold air. Paul followed a long rattle sequence with several raucous clashes before he whispered, "Right!"

Without turning my head, I noticed a shape at the edge of my peripheral vision, then made out the immobile form of a doe standing at the edge of the clearing. Not until she was satisfied that the wind carried no wisps of unwelcome scent did she step forward. Something was behind her, but I couldn't make it out. The next thing I saw was heavy hind quarters disappearing into a brushy draw. When I looked back, the doe had also vanished.

Paul rattled several more times without luck. I had hoped that a big buck would come charging into the clearing or at least try to sneak in. After five minutes, Paul stood up and shrugged his shoulders. I followed as he headed down the road. A shallow draw died in the meadow, and we had just walked around the head of it when Paul suddenly froze. A doe and a buck were streaking across the road, but before I could react, they were swallowed by the thickets. The rack looked heavy and tall.

We just shook our heads. When we checked the tracks, it appeared that the buck had been heading toward Paul's rattling, perhaps following the doe. Unfortunately, when she veered off, the buck didn't take another step in our direction. At least the rattling had attracted a buck, which gave me hope.

We continued following the road for another 10 minutes to a fence line that ran along the edge of a wash. The wash was 50 feet deep with only scattered brush and small trees on either side. I could see well enough to make a several-hundred-yard shot, if I got the chance. It was a perfect place to rattle, so we decided to try our luck again. Backing up to trees, we sat so that we could each watch different approaches and were soon into the rhythm of the rattling series. Paul had smacked the horns together for several minutes when suddenly a deer snorted its warning less than 20 yards behind us. The snow apparently worked as well for the buck as it did for us. He didn't make a sound coming in. By the time I spun around, he was gone. Later Paul told me that he saw the huge body and swollen neck of a rutting buck just before he wheeled to run.

Not everyone was having my kind of luck. Most of the eight hunters in camp when I arrived had tagged out by the fourth day. We were all seeing at least a dozen bucks a day, and several good bucks were missed. I had yet to fire a shot. That night, I couldn't help but think about a call I made to Mike that summer. His crew had already spotted four 160-point-plus bucks in the pastures, and one of the bucks, he said, was a monster. Mike called it "Double Drop," and estimated that it might score over 190 points!

Paul and I had spent time under a rimrock overlooking the brushy draw where they spotted Double Drop. So did the other hunters. We saw a few bucks, and plenty of does, but the big buck had disappeared. Every night we wracked our brains trying to figure out where Double Drop and the other big bucks might have gone during the rut. The next day we needed to try something different. During the past four days we had tried every technique imaginable, including approaching the pastures and surrounding hills from different directions. Nothing. The big bucks had disappeared as completely as if they'd dropped off the face of the earth. The storm, now raging past its fourth day, wasn't helping!

That evening Paul's father, Tim, pulled into camp. He and Paul planned to hunt the last three days of the season together. That night it finally stopped snowing, and the wind died. Tim's timing couldn't have been much better. The deer would be moving, and in combination with the rut, the hunting was going to be dynamite! I was so pumped that I had a tough time sleeping that night. A clear night sky preceded bitter cold and a calm, sunny day for the first time since my hunt dawned. Ice crystals sparkled like diamonds in the light.

Jim Bailey, one of the other experienced guides in camp, had already filled out his other clients. He came into the kitchen that morning to inform me that he had just drawn the "short straw." I jumped into his pickup and we headed to the U2. Over the next few hours, we tried every hunting trick in our tool box—stillhunting, rattling, and glassing. The deer were definitely moving, and by noon we had spotted 17 bucks, including several that would have scored in the 130s. Still no sign of Double Drop or any of the bigger bucks, though.

We had pulled up to the top of a knob that was one of Jimmy's favorites for glassing. It was isolated from the surrounding hills, but gave us a view of several ridges and draws leading away from Fuller pasture. The draws dumped into the river bottom near the main ranch house. It looked like a good travel route between feeding and bedding areas.

I had just finished attaching my binoculars to the tripod when Jimmy exclaimed, "There's a great buck!" I glanced at the buck only long enough to see that he was chasing several does and bluffing a young buck as they crossed a hillside. Dropping my glasses, I jumped up and ran to the truck for my spotting scope. By the time I dug it out of my pack and returned, the buck was gone. Jimmy excitedly told me, "That was the biggest buck I've seen this year," which was good enough for me. He then added fuel, saying, "He has a long drop tine off his right beam." Jimmy also told me that it was the first time that he had seen this buck. That meant there were at least five great whitetail bucks on Mike's leases.

We took a second to get our bearings and locate several landmarks on the sidehill before heading out. We had to cross two ridges before reaching the one where we'd spotted the big buck, but finally we were double-timing it up the last hill. On the way, we bumped a doe and fawn and sighed with relief when both of them ran out of sight at the head of the ridge. As we neared the crest, we slowed down. I didn't want to be gasping for air if the buck was just over the rise. Full of expectations, we crossed the top, but there was no sign of the buck, or for that matter any deer. We dropped back and looped higher up the ridge to try again. This time when we peaked over, a five-point buck was feeding 60 yards away. Something seemed wrong, though, and then I realized that he was a unicorn, so to speak. The left main beam was snapped off just above the pedicle. Another much smaller buck was bedded on the slope behind him, but there was no sign of the big buck. For the next two hours we climbed, circled, and poked into every hiding place we could find without catching sight of that buck. We did find the big splayed-out track of a single deer taking 20- to 30-foot strides, certainly a deer on the run. Something had spooked our buck, perhaps the doe and fawn we bumped earlier, or maybe that strange sixth sense that big bucks seem to have.

That night Tim and three friends of Mike's hauled bucks back to camp. None were huge, just decent trophies scoring up to 140 points. They also reported that deer were moving throughout the day. Paul and I still had tags in our pockets and the last two days of the season left.

Thursday was a mirror of the previous day, clear and cold with a light breeze from the south. Jimmy and I were late getting back to the knob because we kept bumping into deer as we moved along the river bottom on the U2. The best of the bucks wouldn't have scored 130 points. Naturally, one buck watching us from a grove of red oaks would have allowed a dead-sure standing shot. It was mid-morning by the time we reached the knob, and the bright sun was causing us fits. The glare created a glistening mirage that danced over the snow, wavering so badly that I couldn't use my spotting scope even at 20 power, its lowest magnification. Using our binoculars, we spotted 11 small bucks by noon. For several more hours we carefully picked apart all the likely hiding places in the draws and distant pastures near the ranch house, some of them several times. We needed a change.

Ice shattered when our truck plowed through the Belle Fourche River. We climbed out of the river bottom and cottonwoods and headed up the grade to Billfold and Bentonite pastures. Other hunters throughout the week had spotted two exceptional bucks while hunting this area. One had been shot at, so there was no telling where he was hiding, but the other buck had slipped away undisturbed. We drove slowly through both pastures, carefully glassing the surrounding ridges. We saw many does and a few bucks, but darkness found us empty-handed again, driving back down the gravel road to the lodge.

Paul was late arriving, but when he backed his truck into the barn we knew that he was packing meat. He had killed the 4 x 4 in Horse Pasture. The rack was everything we thought, heavy and tall, but it had a bonus 4-inch kicker off the G2 that we hadn't noticed earlier. It was too cold for me to stand out in the barn and measure the rack, but I still felt that we had him pegged with a score in the high 140s. Paul's success left me with the only tag in camp and only one day to fill it.

The question we discussed over coffee the next morning was repetitive: what now? We had tried to find the double-drop buck several times. We had spent many hours near the knob looking for the buck Jimmy spotted. We climbed into The Gap twice to see if bucks were moving on that side of the divide. We had even checked out a number of spots where, in the past, Paul and Jimmy had found bucks. We had, in short, exhausted every logical place where we might find a buck. With a good deal of input from Mike and the other guides, we put together a plan that would see my last morning in Fuller Pasture, later moving to the knob, and then swinging across the river to Billfold for the evening hunt. I hoped I wouldn't get past Fuller Pasture.

Sunrise had just peaked through the clouds hanging over the row of distant mountains when we pulled down the final grade to the U2 ranch. A trail, barely visible in the snow, circled an old corral just off the road then headed up the hill. We had just rounded the corral when Jimmy spotted several does and at least one buck in a patch of oaks on the hill. Unfortunately, I could only see the buck's hindquarters in the trees and only part of his rack. The rest was indistinguishable from the branches. The buck was playing the waiting game; he wasn't about to go off half-cocked and throw caution to the wind. It was a stand-off. The does finally made the decision for all of us when they scrambled for thicker cover taking the buck with them. I caught glimpses of the buck in the trees and brush as he moved steadily up the hill until, finally, he was gone.

Jimmy startled me when he yelled, "Come on, let's go!" We jumped back in the truck and headed for the top, circling around to get the wind right. I quickly found a place to stand with plenty of shooting lanes, including a low pass to my right, which offered a logical crossing. While I got settled in, Jimmy took off around the top of the hill hoping to flank the deer and move them my way. After an hour of standing in the snow, all our plan produced was cold feet. When we joined up again, Jimmy told me that he had cut a lone set of big tracks heading in the opposite direction. The hunter-savvy whitetail had given us the slip. Over the next several hours we saw plenty of bucks, but nothing of any real size. Only an hour and a half was left before darkness would drop the curtain on my season. Time to head for Billfold, the last gasp on our last-day deer plan.

We splashed and crunched across the river, climbed out of the river bottom, and actually stopped on an open sidehill where we could see the head of Billfold. It wasn't long before we were both whispering that we had spotted deer in the trees.

Quietly, Jimmy announced, "There's your buck." He pointed to my left to a stand of ponderosa pines near the top of the pasture. I could see several deer feeding through the trees, but couldn't find a buck. Jimmy was carefully following the buck in his glasses and told me that he was screened behind a tree. Finally, he stepped out, and even at over 800 yards I could clearly see his 5 x 5 frame. The tines weren't as long as I had hoped, but with only minutes to go in the season, he was certainly good enough.

We hastily formulated a stalk, which neither of us liked, but the wind direction and the remaining time wouldn't let us get fancy. Grabbing my rifle and binoculars, we dove into the ravine, heading straight at the herd. For the few minutes it took to drop off the hill, we would be in plain sight. Just before we reached the bottom, I checked one more time to make sure that the deer were still feeding. We hustled for the next hundred yards before we went into first gear and started the final leg of our stalk. Working uphill quietly, I thought we were still well short of the feeding herd when I glanced to my left and was stunned to see a deer only 30 yards away. She had us dead to rights, but luckily was feeding and looking away. We pulled in beside a bush and waited...and waited...and waited. Finally, the doe fed into the trees, and we squirmed ahead.

I was getting nervous. Light was fading fast. As we kept working our way uphill toward the pines, we kept glassing ahead hoping that the buck would feed across the slope. Instead, it became obvious after 10 minutes that the herd had continued up the ridge. Doing our best Delta Force imitation, we advanced tree-to-tree, covering another 100 yards. It was almost dark, and we still hadn't found the big buck. Other deer kept coming up the slope, each time nailing us down for precious minutes until they passed. Several were small bucks, so I didn't even consider pulling the trigger.

Just after we left the truck, the question flashed through my mind, "Is this going to be another last-minute buck?" Everything pointed to that possibility. But now, on this last day of November on a lonely hillside in a quiet, snowy corner of Wyoming, Lady Luck stood me up.

I was lying on the snow-covered ground when we conceded that it was just too dark to shoot and that we were beaten. Rolling over, I sat up and relived in my mind, for a moment, some of the bucks that I let walk and wondered, "What if?"

This was my second whitetail hunt with Trophies Plus Outfitters, and I have yet to pull the trigger. In fact, I was the only hunter two years in a row who didn't. Still, I'd seen and passed on at least six bucks that would score 130 points and higher and had a couple of close brushes with record-book bucks! I'll keep coming back as long as there are bucks like Double Drop, Jimmy's big buck, the ghostly 5 x 5 in Horse Pasture, and a great buck that a friend of mine, Jim McCarthy, shot several weeks before my arrival. I'm already planning my return bout. Perhaps, next time I'll break my jinx.

Tough
Hunts for
Kansas
Whitetails

I BREATHED a sigh of relief when my flight finally landed in Wichita and all of my hunting gear slid down the baggage chute. I was already two days late for my September muzzle-loader hunt with Stan and Mary Jones of Eight Mile Outfitters. Just getting here had been a nightmare of cancelled flights, backed up terminals, and three flight changes within eight hours. It felt so good to actually be starting my long-anticipated whitetail hunt that I wasn't even discouraged when I stepped out of the airport terminal into the 90-degree temperature, thick and heavy with oppressive humidity. The heat hit me like a fist. A day before, I'd been in the cold and wet of Kodiak, Alaska, and my body's thermostat was still set on Sitka blacktail country with its high basins and frigid saltwater fjords.

When I pulled into his yard, Stan was skinning one of two whitetail bucks that had been tagged by representatives from the Cabela's hunting team. The racks on both bucks scored over 150 points, reinforcing the glowing stories my friend, Cliff Graham of Associated Hunting Consultants, had told me about Stan's whitetail operation. During the previous season, even bigger bucks had been taken on Eight Mile Outfitters' leases, and I had fantasies about whacking one of those monster-racked whitetails for my Deer Quest.

Cliff was a widely experienced whitetail hunter from Pennsylvania and was scheduled to join me in camp. It was encouraging, because with his connections, he could hunt with any number of trophy whitetail outfitters. Other hunters were filtering back to camp, giving me a chance to meet everyone and catch up on what I'd missed the first two days. The big story around the dinner table that evening involved well-known writer and editor, Bill Bynum. His story turned out to be a not-so-funny example of why it's important to be in the right place at the right time, but the events of his trip won't be soon forgotten. Any hunter who has had a close call with a lifetime dream could identify with his tale.

Bill's saga started that morning when Kevin Shafer, a Pennsylvanian hunter, had watched two good bucks feed in a soybean field safely beyond muzzleloader range. Eventually, the deer fed onto a small rise in the field and bedded down. Rather than attempt a tricky, open-field stalk, Kevin waited until noon to meet Bill, another hunter, Kenneth Boster, and guide Bob Beardslee.

The plan was to surround the bean field and simultaneously move in on the bedded bucks. They hoped that someone would get

Cliff Graham is smiling after he connected on this eight-pointer during his September muzzleloader hunt.

a shot before the bucks made it to cover. Everyone moved into position and started their stalk. Bill was moving between the soybean rows when he noticed that the plants ahead were bent in an odd manner. His hunting instincts immediately kicked in. His pace slowed, eyes sharpened, and senses peaked. Muzzleloader ready, Bill advanced a half step at a time, moving quietly, bent low, following the tilled row, and carefully moving the plants aside with his legs.

The closer he approached, the more convinced he was that the bucks were bedded in the beans just ahead. Slowly, silently, he advanced until suddenly he spotted tines above the low plants. The soybeans offered both a plus and minus. The minus was that Bill couldn't see the racks well enough to tell how big the bucks were. On the plus side, the soybeans were high enough to restrict the vision of the bedded bucks to a narrow tunnel. By keeping low, Bill slipped unseen to within 15 yards. The bucks, he said, were relaxed and had no idea danger was close. Raising his muzzleloader, Bill calmly slipped off the safety and whistled softly. The nearest buck stood up, looked into the business end of the muzzleloader, and left. Bill didn't shoot! The little that he could see of the other buck's rack was enough to make him hold off.

Inexplicably, the second buck stayed in its bed, but stretched its neck to see what caused all the fuss. Incredibly, after a few tense seconds, it relaxed. Bill waited a moment, then inched to within five yards. By now he was so close Bill had his smokepole pointed down. He collected himself, paused, and then softly said, "Hey!" The surprised buck lumbered to its feet, stood stock still for a second, and then trotted off.

It was like shooting fish in a barrel. Bill held dead on, and, as any good marksman is trained to do, squeezed the trigger.

Nothing!

He pulled it hard.

Nothing!

Frantic now, he yanked it not once, but several times, as his frustration mounted.

Nothing!

The buck nonchalantly trotted down the rise, crossed the field, and disappeared into the trees. Behind it, skylined on a slight rise in a soybean field, 15 feet from a still-warm buck bed, stood a frustrated gun writer with a prototype muzzleloader that refused to fire. Three other hunters were standing nearby staring with utter amazement. No one shot!

That night Bill was sick as he related his sad story. How big were the bucks? Opinions varied slightly, but the consensus of the rest of the crew that watched the saga unfold was that the "small" buck would have scored at least 160 points. The big boy, they thought, would have scored 190 points, and possibly more. Bill said the buck was easily the biggest buck he's ever had a chance to shoot and maybe ever will.

After all the stories of bucks seen, and some missed, I couldn't wait to start my hunt. Still, my next morning's hunt was a bust. I saw three bucks, but they weren't what I'd traveled all the way from Oregon to tag. I passed the time sitting in the blind thinking about Bill's big buck.

Not a breath of air was moving, and the thermometer in Stan's garage read 92 degrees as I headed to my stand in the afternoon. The East Canyon blind overlooked a coulee leading to fields of milo and corn where bucks often fed at night. Perched just under the skyline, the closed blind overlooked promising openings in the brush. A feeder was several hundred yards away in the bottom of the ravine, well beyond range of my muzzleloader. I didn't want to kill my whitetail over a feeder anyway. Stan assured me that the bigger bucks weren't using feeders, preferring the rich field browse instead.

It takes special discipline to be a good stand hunter and stay alert at all times. Nod off, even for a second, and the big one will cross the shooting lane and be gone. I was determined not to let that happen to me. Still, I find that sitting at full attention for long periods is tough on an old mule deer hunter who rarely sits any longer than it takes to glass a likely area. The warm sun beat on the blind, insects buzzed, and I had to open the windows to stay alert. True to his prediction, just before dark a half-dozen small three-and four-point bucks slipped into the coulee headed toward the fields.

It was after dark when Stan parked his rig at the top of the hill to pick me up. He was late, he explained, because he was watching two bucks in one of his pastures bordering the highway. Stan told me that he loses big bucks from that pasture to road-hunting poachers and to a neighbor who kills any buck that wanders onto his farm. Stan prefers to keep the bucks out of that pasture, even if it means that they are spooked for a couple days.

When our headlights swept across the field, Stan spotted a buck moving along a shallow ravine. The buck was on the driver's side. I couldn't get a good look, but Stan thought that it was one of several bigger bucks he had been watching all summer. When the lights hit him, the buck disappeared before we could get a good look. In the half-light shadows at the edge of our headlight beams, however, a second buck hid behind a screen of brush. In my glasses, it appeared that the rack had several stickers and high tines coming off long main beams. I wanted to see more detail, but when we moved closer, this buck followed the other out of the pasture. The memory of those two bucks helped me pass many boring hours in the blinds over the next few days, while sitting idly waiting for those few seconds of pandemonium.

Driving around that day, it was easy to see firsthand what Cliff had meant when he told me that Stan and Mary weren't "typical Kansas farmers and part-time hunting outfitters." On earlier Kansas whitetail expeditions I had hunted on other farms with big bucks, but those bucks weren't there because of anything the farmer did. Those so-called outfitters were farmers first and foremost, and secondarily were outfitters who took a few weeks off to guide hunters. Stan and Mary, on the other hand, are part-time farmers and full-time outfitters. Stan farms only if there is no work to do on the outfitting end of the business. Both Stan and Mary are committed to their outfitting business and to managing the land for trophy whitetails.

They use strip and contour farming techniques, while planting as many as 10 different whitetail foods, each maturing at different times of the year. In addition, they plant many food plots on slivers of acreages tucked away in small openings in woodlands or between hedgerows, as well as fields covering many acres. They have also developed many water sources.

Stan invests a lot of time looking for promising new leases in the best units in Kansas. He is an avid archer who carefully scouts every farm with a hunter's eye before leasing. Stan looks for exceptional herd genetics and the land's potential for developing quality whitetails. After leasing a farm, he improves the natural potential by installing feeders and paying the farmer to leave standing grain crops unharvested as additional food sources.

The work doesn't stop with food sources and water. I am amazed at the number of blinds that Stan has positioned on his farm, as well as on his leased land. He uses a thick notebook binder crammed with topographical maps to explain the locations of blinds to his hunters. There are more than 50 hydraulic stands and nearly that many fixed blinds that Stan places months ahead of the hunting seasons. In addition, there are numerous tree stands and ground blinds located at strategic locations. It's a full-time job just maintaining that many blinds, let alone the last-minute adjustments made throughout the season.

Stan nurtures close working relationships with the other farmers in the area, and it paid off after dinner on my second night in camp. A neighboring farmer called to report that he had spotted a good buck that evening running along a creek bottom on one of Stan's leases. I could sense the excitement in Stan's voice when he told me that he had a hunch the buck carried one of the largest whitetail racks in the area. Twice during the summer he had spotted the buck, and Stan told me that he was huge. I was the only hunter in camp with a tag for the unit. You can guess where I was headed the next morning.

Stan drove me out into the field long before the trees were silhouetted in the coming light. His instructions seemed simple. Cross the plowed field to the tree line, turn left, and follow it until it turned south, walk another quarter mile, cross the creek, and look for a hydraulic blind overlooking a small meadow. Everything went as planned until I got to the creek. Instead of the jumpable creek that I expected, I discovered a slough and found out the hard way that the water was calf high. Boots and pants already soaked, I waded across and soon was sitting in an open blind 20 feet above the meadow. When it got light enough that I could see details on the ground around me, I was shocked to see that the creek behind me was dry!

In the dark I had blundered into a slough that was only 50 yards long and the only water within two miles. Just my luck! On the far side of the meadow, a low rise covered in oaks and other hardwoods separated my meadow from the milo field above. It wasn't long before a small forked-horn buck materialized out of the trees and walked into the opening before it started feeding. He was soon joined by three more small bucks. Although the rut was months away, the bucks were already establishing dominance, ganging up on the smallest buck and pushing him all over the meadow. One would stop pushing, and the next buck would take his turn. The mock battles lasted a half-hour. Unfortunately, the skirmishes provided my only excitement that morning. At noon, Stan showed up in the Suburban. This time, when I left the field, I walked across the dry stream bed and skirted the slough.

I paid attention to tracks on my way out. The big buck was using a hedgerow as a concealed travel lane extending on south of the milo fields. When I told Stan about what I found, he recommended that I set up an ambush in an established archery stand in the tree line. Early that afternoon we drove to the south end of the hedgerow. I would have plenty of time to get settled before deer started moving.

When I reached the stand, I began to understand why Stan had asked me if I would be comfortable using an archery stand. At the time, I didn't understand the importance of the question. I do now. The narrow stand was high in a dead tree with a ladder that swung free similar to climbing a rope ladder. The tree swayed as I climbed and continued to sway while I sat on the 12-inch seat. No danger of falling asleep in this stand! I have been in worse blinds, but it gave me something to kid Stan about later. He listened patiently while I gave him a bad time, and then shot back a simple question, "Did you see any bucks?"

He knew, of course, that I had seen three four-pointers and two smaller bucks before dark. One buck was decent, and I had carefully looked him over as he fed in the milo 40 yards away. I guessed that the 4 x 4 rack would score in the mid-140s; a nice buck, but too small to shoot for my quest.

Before the 140-plus buck stepped out into the field, I heard a racket farther down the hedgerow. I was staring into the thick cover when a small 4 x 4 buck exploded out of it on a dead run. The panicked buck zipped past my blind and disappeared so fast it would have been a miracle if I had gotten a shot off. The noise had hardly died away when another 4 x 4 buck hot on his trail charged directly under my stand. The last buck must have been quicker, because it wasn't long before they were banging heads deep in the cover; then it was strangely silent. It was an entertaining, but unproductive evening.

I was starting to get nervous. The only real shooters that I had spotted had been the two big pasture bucks in the headlights my first night. God only knows where those bucks were now. Unlike me, the big bucks had the good sense to bed during the day tucked away deep in cover, not coming out until the last fringe of shooting light. I had one day left to hunt. Things didn't look good!

While driving to my blind the next morning, Stan surprised me with the information that if my hunt didn't pan out with my muzzleloader, my landowner tag would still allow me to hunt with a center-fire rifle during the December season. While we were talking, I couldn't help but think about the two racks back in camp. These were magnum bucks that Mary and Stan's father, Harry, killed during the rifle season the previous year. Their racks were convincing evidence that December might be a winner.

I still hadn't snapped a cap when Stan returned to my blind after dark on that last day of my muzzleloader hunt. On our way back to camp, I made arrangements to return in December packing my

7mm magnum. There was one complication. Because my Wyoming hunt ended on the last day of November, I would arrive four days late for the opening of rifle season.

A Rifle in the Winter

This time when my airliner landed in Kansas, the sweltering 90-plus temperatures that had greeted my first landing had at least cooled off, but not by much. However, it was better than the snow whipping around the airport parking lot in Rapid City, South Dakota, when I left. In Kansas I could expect unseasonably warm weather and, at times, plenty of wind. I smiled and guessed that I wouldn't need my cold weather gear that I was still packing from my Wyoming hunt.

Mary met me at the airport, and our drive back to camp was filled with stories of the earlier archery hunts and the first four days of rifle hunts. I was surprised to hear that Bill Bynum's buck had escaped again. A rifle hunter had a crack at him, but didn't connect. Talk about a charmed life! Stan and Mary, of course, were as disappointed as the luckless shooter. The big whitetail would have improved a season marred by muzzleloader malfunctions, missed shots, hot weather, and several wounded bucks. On the bright side, I was happy that Scott Olmsted, Executive Editor of *American Hunter* magazine, whom I had met during muzzleloader season, was also back in camp. He had a permit for a different unit so we couldn't hunt together, but his hunting stories helped make our evenings interesting.

I also anticipated talking with two other buddies. Tony Lee, an old friend and Alaskan outfitter with whom I had hunted 15 years earlier, was supposed to be in camp along with outfitter friend, Chris Loncarich, a noted cat hunter from Colorado. Unfortunately for me, but boding well for the hunt, I learned that Chris had tagged his buck the first day and had already returned to Colorado. After dinner Tony told me that both mornings he had passed shots on a buck at least as big as the ones already in camp. Those were big bucks. Reports like that helps build my confidence!

The faint crimson of coming light was barely visible as once again I was sitting in the blind overlooking East Canyon. No one had been in the blind since a hunter shot a buck there on opening morning of the rifle season. Just as they were doing during muzzle-loader season, bucks were still using the canyon as a route to food plots one-half mile away.

It wasn't long before the first buck showed up, but not where I expected. It came out of a field on the opposite rim of the draw and was well down into one of the brushy side draws before I picked him up. My rangefinder put him at 410 yards. I quickly arranged the sandbags that Stan kept in his blinds, not unlike those I had used for months on the shooting range. My 400-yard stadia hair was rock solid on the buck's shoulder.

The buck was partially hidden, moving and feeding through the brush, and tough to see in the indirect early light, even with the 20-power scope. My breathing was coming more rapidly. I

Scott Olmsted killed this fine ten-point whitetail when he returned for the December rifle hunt. He has a right to be happy!

couldn't see much of the rack, but what I did see looked good. A small clearing ahead of the buck offered my best chance for a clear shot. I set up there. When the maybe-buck stepped out, I could instantly see that it was a young 3 x 3. Its G2s were at least 8-inches long, and the G3s were only slightly shorter, but the thin main beams were well inside its ears. In a few years, this buck was going to be outstanding, but he still had some growing to do. Settling back into my seat, I let my pulse return to normal.

Suddenly, I noticed a buck not 100 yards away. It slipped in while I was concentrating on the other buck. This buck was moving slowly down the canyon, pausing to snatch an occasional morsel. A doe followed close behind. It didn't take a second to see that it was a nice 4 x 4 with a kicker. Both back tines were longer than the ears and the beams stretched well out over its nose. The 3-inch tine that came off the G3 was shorter than the eye guard's. I was adding figures in my mind and came up with 145 points. Now I was talking to myself. Do I or don't I?

Both sides of my brain were debating the question when the buck changed direction and walked straight toward my blind. When he was 30 yards away, I certainly didn't need binoculars. I had already turned my scope power down. As I tracked the buck in the scope, it dawned on me that if I squeezed the trigger, I would break one of my cardinal rules. Years ago, experience taught me that a truly big buck makes your mind scream "Shoot!" When I have to talk myself into shooting, I am better off passing and hoping for a better one. That rule had served me well over the years and often produced much bigger bucks than those I passed. Once again, I tossed the dice and gave the buck a walk. I had four more days to hunt and still hoped to find a buck like Bynum's.

Two days later I was kicking myself. I was seeing at least six bucks each day, but still hadn't looked down my rifle barrel at a big buck. At breakfast Stan told me to pack my gear. I was being sent south to the far end of Unit 15, beyond reasonable daily driving distance. I was to meet one of Stan's young guides, Billy Hamill, who lived in the small town of Anthony. A local motel would be home for the last two days of my hunt, and I would eat dinners at a local restaurant. The move meant missing Mary's wonderful meals, but the sacrifice would be worth it if I tagged a big buck.

I met Billy in front of his father's butcher shop shortly after lunch. Both of them are avid hunters, and their photo albums prove it. Billy is a bow hunter and had already shot several bucks that most of us only dream about. His best whitetail scored 186 Pope & Young points.

Billy reported spotting a great buck two days earlier near an abandoned windmill at the head of a huge field. That's where he wanted me sitting. Over the next two days, I got well acquainted with that windmill's platform, as well as every bush within sight. What I didn't see was that big buck. Fresh tracks each morning confirmed that deer were indeed feeding in the field at my back, but the trophy buck never showed. During daylight only a couple of does ventured into the open.

Another of Stan's hunters, Jim Crawford, sitting in a blind to the north, was luckier. He saw a buck that he felt would score in the 160s and videotaped him instead of making the stalk and shooting. I was shaking my head as he told us the story. After I left, Jim did not find the buck he wanted; although he saw several bucks most of us would consider shooters.

At the end of my last full day, I wasn't sorry to leave the windmill and the motel. It was long after dark when I pulled into Stan's yard. I still had the morning to hunt before driving to Wichita to catch my flight home.

Stan dropped me at the East Canyon blind one last time and promised to pick me up before noon to get on the road to the airport no later than 1:00 p.m. Again, I saw bucks, but the best was one of the small 3 x 4s that I passed earlier.

Waiting in the blind gave me time to come to grips with the realization that my last chance to kill a whitetail was over. I had already decided that my plans for this book would have to be put on hold. I tried dwelling on the positives—the trophies that I had already shot and the beautiful country I had hunted.

I was still looking forward to my hunts for Coues and desert mule deer in Mexico. In short, I had accepted the fact that my quest for all six deer varieties was unsuccessful and I had already moved on.

Noon came and went, and I was getting anxious to return to the house. I still had to do my last-minute packing and change for my flight home. I was reasonably sure that non-hunters on the plane wouldn't appreciate my scent-covered camo, although I chuckled at the thought. Finally, one of Stan's helpers, Frank Salisbury, pulled up and I jumped into his truck. He apologized and told me that Stan had been delayed on one of his other leases. We were busy chatting as we pulled up to the last gate.

Suddenly a doe broke out of a hedgerow across the field to our left, followed closely by a buck with his neck stretched out, trying his best to catch her. Luckily, my binoculars were still hanging around my neck, but I only caught glimpses of the buck's rack as he raced across the field in hot pursuit. Both deer easily cleared the fence on their way toward Stan's house.

"Come on," Frank yelled, "I think I know where they are going." We jumped back into the truck and rocketed down Stan's gravel entrance road for a quarter mile. Frank braked, and we bailed out. Sure enough, the doe appeared in an old farm road leading to the fields behind Stan's barn. Warily, she stopped to look before crossing. I had just enough time to get my rifle up when the buck stepped out. He looked at us for a second and then at the doe, reluctant to leave her. She finally had enough, however, and wheeled to dive back into the cover. He was following when I pulled the trigger.

The bullet delivered its lethal blow, and the buck skidded to a stop at the base of an oak tree. "Victory had been snatched out of the jaws of defeat" with less than two minutes to go in my hunt. I had shot without getting a good look at the rack. While we were flying down the gravel road, we had estimated that the buck might score in the 140s.

Frank and I didn't waste a step while covering the 100 yards to the downed buck. It took a few moments for the realization to sink in of how lucky I was even to be standing over the whitetail that filled the slot in my Deer Quest. I was just as happy with my last-minute buck as if he had scored much higher.

Time was now critical. Scott and several other hunters were already packed and waiting to leave. We took a couple photos and left on a dead run. Frank agreed to take care of the meat while I packed. I wasn't able to measure the rack until Stan shipped it to me. Several months later the 3 x 4 rack measured 132-3/8 points.

Admittedly, it was smaller than my goal of 160 points, but I didn't care because I knew before I started that my goals were lofty. They were, instead, meant to increase the challenge of my quest, and they certainly did. Besides, my goals were never meant to be a win-lose proposition. However, after 22 days of hunting whitetails, spanning four months in Wyoming and Kansas, I'll admit that I cut it too close!

The author's nine-point whitetail buck appeared at the last possible moment.

Mexico's
"Other"
Whitetail

I WAS SQUIRMING trying to find a soft rock as I sat glassing a nameless hill in northern Sonora, Mexico. After an hour, every pebble had left an indelible impression in my "mind." Uncomfortable as I was, I wasn't about to leave. Somewhere on that hill a monster Coues deer buck was tucked away into the mixed ocotillo, cactus, and scrub oak. Aptly nicknamed the "gray ghost," no other deer in North America can disappear as well into so little. Successful hunters learn to slow down and then go even slower. Patience is a great virtue for hunting these little whitetails, but unfortunately that's not one of my strongest suits.

Kirk Kelso, owner of Pusch Ridge Outfitters, and my guide, José Valencia, were sitting to my left staring into their tripod-mounted binoculars also trained on the hillside. We have hunted together so often that I knew that they weren't going to miss much. Earlier, their sharp eyes had picked out several average-rack bucks, but not the one I had traveled several thousand miles to find. Only a few days before, Kirk had spotted a buck in this canyon that he claimed would score 110 points, maybe slightly better.

I had just readjusted the tripod legs and cinched down the quick release toggle on my 15-power binoculars when I noticed movement at the top of a cliff more than a thousand yards away. While I was focusing the glasses, the distant shape moved several yards and was joined by another black shape. This one I could see well enough to identify it as a javelina.

I casually mentioned, "javelina," when something a lot bigger shot out of the cover. It took me more time to yell, "lion" than it did for the cougar to disappear. It was making tracks! As I called out directions to Kirk and José, the lion easily covered 100 yards with a dozen javelina in hot pursuit. The cougar obviously didn't want anything to do with that many flashing tusks. With ground-eating bounds, the big cat easily outdistanced the herd then shot up a lone mesquite tree that clung precariously to the side of a rugged 20-foot cliff. With our powerful glasses, we could clearly see the lion stretched out on a gnarled limb, its long tail nervously swishing its disapproval. The javelinas scrambled through the rocks, frantic to find a way to get to the cat—just daring him to come down. We guessed that the cougar had attacked one of the javelina before the herd turned on him.

This was the fifth mountain lion that I had seen in the last three years of hunting in Sonora with Kirk. And for the third time, I declined the stalk. Somewhere on that mountain was a potential record-book Coues deer buck, a trophy that I had tried for years to tag. I was beginning to think that when it came to killing a large Coues deer, I was "snakebit." Over the last dozen years other hunters in my camps had taken huge bucks, and my perennial lack of success was becoming a sore spot, my Achilles heel; certainly, one not missed by Kirk and his camp manager, Tom "Pancho" Phillips. They didn't waste many chances to good-naturedly remind me of my shortcoming. I had taken "camp rat" honors so many times I was even beginning to believe that I might deserve the title.

But this was my year! I could feel in my hunter's soul that I was finally going to break my string of bad luck. Dropping a record-book Coues buck would not only get these guys off my back, but it would be a fitting addition to my Deer Quest. I had set my sights on killing a Coues buck that would score 100 points or higher, but frankly, I hoped to pick up some extra points to help make up for my Kansas whitetail. Kirk's buck would fit the bill nicely!

Kirk specializes in finding big Coues deer and I was encouraged by his description of the buck he spotted earlier in this area. Head guide, Jim Reynolds, told me that he had also seen the buck and felt that it would score at least 110 points. Jim has more trophy

The author's Coues deer buck's long, bladed main beams are what convinced his guides that this buck would "book." Both 18-inch plus beams were trying to split again making them heavy out to their ends.

Coues bucks to his credit than anyone I know and, when it comes to hunting these little deer, he knows what he is doing. Unfortunately, Jim was running another one of Kirk's Coues deer camps farther south and would not be available to help me. Kirk told me that when he and Jim saw the buck, they were guiding a client who missed it. Obviously, finding the buck was going to be only one of the challenges to hanging him on my wall.

Three other hunters joined me in camp on that December hunt. Bill Hober, CEO of Swift Bullet Company, and his guest, Jim Carmichel, Shooting Editor for *Outdoor Life*, had both previously killed Coues deer scoring over 100 points. They were looking for something better. My hunting partner, Dave Lechel, had killed smaller bucks and now had his sights set on a buck that would score at least 100 points. It was a tall order to find four bucks to match our "wish list!" After all, 100 points was the minimum for B&C Awards record book recognition.

When I was setting up my hunt, Kirk had assured me that "book bucks" could be found on Rancho Guarachi and the surrounding ranches where he leased hunting rights. All we had to do, he said, was find one.

The evening custom in most Mexican hunting camps is for the hunters and guides to congregate around a campfire to spin tales and tell jokes. Fueled by dry mesquite or ironwood snags, the flickering light is bewitching, and its warmth takes the edge off the evening chill. However, on our first night in camp, we spun our stories almost standing in the fire, crowding close to the flames to ward off a freezing cold driven by a brisk wind. It was ominous hunting weather.

The next morning, the weather was even worse. A howling wind penetrated to my bones. Kirk told me that we would be hunting with Dave and his guide, Alejandro (Alex) Valencia, José's brother. This young man not only has two of the sharpest eyes of any guide I've hunted with, but he is what Kirk calls a "killer." Rarely does Alex make a stalk that doesn't end with blood on his hands. By mutual agreement, the first 100-plus buck we found that day was to be Dave's shot.

My partner's chance came as we were driving to one of Kirk's favorite lookouts. We spotted several Coues deer above the rugged trail as we rounded a sharp corner.

After jumping out of the Suburban, all we could see were glimpses of a good buck working its way through the brush up the steep slope.

Kirk was pleading with Dave to, "Hurry, get ready!" Dave pulled down his bipod and was scurrying to find a shooting position for a target that was sharply uphill and three football fields away. Watching Dave was almost comical. He had three choices—all bad. The bipod legs were too short to accommodate the steep uphill shot. If he went prone and squeezed one off, the recoil at such a sharp angle was guaranteed to leave a "scope smile." His best chance was an off-hand shot, but at 300 yards on a moving buck that wasn't a good choice either. Before we could figure it out, the buck escaped. It was a lucky day—for the buck—and, as it would turn out, for Dave.

Late that evening, Bill Hober pulled into camp with a beautiful buck. Tom, Bill, Jim, and their guides had driven to the northwest corner of the ranch, and it wasn't long before they were into bucks. Bill busted his 4 x 4 buck with one of his company's Scirocco bullets, and all that remained was the hard work. The antlers' green scored 115-2/8 points and netted almost 112 points. After the required drying period, it would be a sure candidate for Boone & Crockett. I secretly begrudged the fact that it probably put him out of contention for "camp rat."

After midnight the din of rain on the tin roof of our sleeping quarters announced the arrival of the storm that had been threatening since I got into camp. My heart sank; hunting had been hard enough in the cold and wind that was pushing ahead of the storm front, but with the arrival of driving rain, the thin-skinned little whitetails would surely hole up.

Kirk informed me that he, José, and I were going to hike to the other side of the hill beyond where we watched the lion and javelinas. Kirk thought that there was a chance the cougar had pushed the big buck into some rough country far beyond the road. Alex and Dave would take the Suburban and hunt in another part of the ranch. Rain splattered on the windshield as we drove toward the hill, and I was really regretting my decision to not pack rain gear for this hunt. I should have had more sense, but after all, this was Mexico! Wind, cold, rain, and no rain gear—all the ingredients for a miserable day were in place when we stepped out of the truck.

On the upside, after five months of almost non-stop hunting, I was in my best physical shape of the last decade. I couldn't help but smile as we fairly flew down the ridge, crossed a deep draw, and climbed up past where we had watched the lion. On the way up, we walked into the middle of the javelina herd. Black pigs snorted, squealed, and flushed in every direction. It scared the hell out of me, but it was proof that we were slipping through the cover silently. The rain quit while we hiked, and, except for every bush being soaked with water, the day and our prospects seemed

A typical lunch on a Sonora hunt includes reheated tortillas with beef and beans, a cool cerveza, and jalapeño peppers.

brighter. Already the clouds were showing promise of letting the sunshine through, and the wind had died.

At the top, we sat down at the first promising overlook and started glassing. To the south, rugged ridges covered with mixed oak, mesquite, and ocotillo looked like perfect big-buck country. Green patches of grass in the deep canyons betrayed seeps. We could see deer feeding on the hillsides, including several bucks in the 100-point range. Kirk kept assuring me that there was a better buck somewhere below us. By 8:30 a.m., it was beginning to warm and streaks of sun shot through the clouds. If we were going to get a crack at Kirk's monster buck, our best chance was to locate him, watch him bed, and plan our stalk. We had to hurry and find him while he was up and feeding, because it would be a great deal harder when he bedded down in the heavy cover.

I had been glassing for only a few minutes when I picked up a decent buck standing in heavy brush. The deer was in the shade of a ridge and already moving toward his bedding area. Kirk put his spotting scope on him, zoomed in and confirmed that it was "just another 100-plus buck." Thirty seconds later, he calmly announced, "There's your buck!"

The buck and a smaller one were feeding on a bench between two ridges one-half mile away. He looked good in my 15-power glasses, but we didn't take long to admire him. There were several options for the stalk. We could cross to the ridge where the 100-point buck was bedded and hope to sneak past without spooking him. That would allow us to follow the ridge to where it ended above the bench within easy shooting distance of the big buck. However, the odds of being able to slip past the bedded buck in the thick brush without spooking it were long.

That prompted us to consider the second alternative. We would have to work down our ridge to a knob below. From our vantage point, it looked like the knob was above the buck's bench and would present a long, but clear shot. If we had misjudged, and the knob was actually below the bench, however, we would probably be unable to see the buck. It was important to move quickly, but at the same time we couldn't risk spooking another deer. The knob was only 400 yards away, and we lost altitude fast as we moved down the spine of the ridge.

I was concerned. If we found ourselves too low to see the buck behind the intervening ridge, we would have to go straight at the bench, but without the advantage of being able to look down into the thickets. That would make it more tricky to spot the deer and even more difficult to crank off a solid shot before he saw us. I much preferred the long shot!

I shouldn't have worried. When we crawled through the last patch of oak and ocotillo, we could still see the buck and his buddy feeding at the far end of the bench. As I prepared for the shot, José and Kirk were whispering to each other, trading comments about the buck. The angle of the slope required extending my bipod to its second stage. After using two of our day packs to prop up the butt of the rifle stock, I had a solid hold. It's times like this that the 20-power rifle scope pays off. The deer's body looked as big as a 100-yard target on my rifle range at home. As I reached up to adjust my scope's parallax, Kirk was reading his Geovid rangefinder. Smiling, he called it at, "exactly 350 yards!" That's point-blank range for my rifle.

While preparing for a shot, I try never to look at antlers that might distract my concentration from the target area on the body. That discipline has paid dividends over the years. With practiced rhythm, the main duplex crosshair settled just under the top of his shoulder. When I touched the trigger I knew that the shot was good, but had lost sight when rocked by the recoil. "What happened?" I blurted. Kirk calmly reached over and slapped me on the head. "He's dead," he announced. My trust in Kirk's judgment and the long-range glimpse of the buck was all the proof I needed to believe that we had a good buck down.

It always takes too long to get to a downed trophy, but this time I deliberately slowed down to calm myself while Kirk and José hurried ahead. I was actually a little sad. It was only my third day, and I was already tagged out. Kirk and José were standing over the buck, when I arrived, admiring the heavy rack. "He's bladed clean out to the end of his main beams," Kirk said. But still he couldn't pass the chance for a little jab when he snipped, "Why did you hit him so high?" I just shook my head. High? The entry hole was easily a third of the way down the shoulder.

We took photos and field dressed the buck. The hardest part of the hunt was still ahead. It was going to be a 3-1/2- to 4-mile hike out of the canyon through some mean, rugged country. The weather was socking in again, and I was hoping that we could get out without getting soaked.

José quickly improvised a sling using the deer's legs. Slashing the thin skin behind the buck's front hocks allowed him to feed the back legs through the slots. He shouldered the buck like a backpack, slinging it over his back with its legs wrapped over his shoulders. Amazingly, José stopped for only three short breaks during that long hike to the hacienda courtyard. One tough hombre!

Returning to camp in early afternoon, we had enough daylight to get the buck skinned, caped, and the meat hung. It was much

Preparing for the shot, the author's prone position and well supported rifle produces a rock-solid hold.

better than the usual knife work at night in the weak light from a kerosene lantern. Arriving early also gave Kirk a chance to measure my buck. We both knew that the tines were too short to "book," so I wasn't surprised with Kirk's verdict of 106-1/8 points. It was my fifth buck with a score high enough to qualify for B&C Award's recognition, but I can't seem to beat their All-Time record book minimum of 110 points. Still, it was a hell of a buck; larger than most Coues deer hunters see in a lifetime. Not only did he beat my Deer Quest goal, but I was feeling pretty confident that I would finally be able to escape my old nemesis—"camp rat" honors.

In the middle of the night I stepped outside and was greeted rudely by snow, wind and a penetrating cold. I had to laugh. I'd traveled thousands of miles from the winter cold in Oregon expecting to enjoy warm Mexican weather. Instead, I find the snow that I thought I'd left at home, which is where my cold weather gear was still stored in a bedroom closet. It looked like I could count on freezing my butt off the next morning when we would be trying to find a buck for Dave.

As we pulled out of the courtyard, Kirk had a lot more confidence than I did. There was a solid blanket of snow covering the ground, and the plants were all bent to the ground with their heavy loads. I knew that it would be even worse on top of the mesa, where we were headed. We could deal with the snow, but what bothered me most was that although we delayed an extra hour longer in camp, the fog was so thick we couldn't see 200 yards. Intermittently, it was still spitting snow. Kirk reminded me that he had killed his biggest Coues buck in snow.

We turned the hubs to kick in the four-wheel drive and clawed our way up a series of rugged canyons topping out on a long mesa with draws leading away in all directions. Each of the draws contained deer, but not many, and by noon we still hadn't found Dave's 100-plus buck. As we dropped off the end of the mesa, Dave was riding shotgun when he spotted a buck racing along the canyon wall. Bailing out, Kirk immediately saw that the buck wouldn't come close to 100 points and took the opportunity to look around. He turned his binoculars to the south, hesitated for a second, and said, "Lance, look at this one!" He jabbed a finger in the general direction of the buck while scrambling to grab his spotting scope from the back of the Suburban.

I slid in behind the tripod and in a split-second spotted one of the best Coues bucks I'd ever laid eyes on. The whitetail was working downhill and would soon be out of our sight behind an intervening ridge. In the background, I could hear Kirk give a simple order, "Go kill that buck!" Reluctantly, I made way for Dave to get a quick peek. Already, Kirk was getting nervous. He assured Dave that the buck would score "at least 105 points," and once more urged him to "Hurry!"

Alex and José would lead the charge down the mountain and up the other side. Kirk and I would stay at the vehicle and work as spotters to guide them into position for a shot. They were supposed to glass back toward us occasionally for hand signals. I was having so much fun watching the buck in the spotting scope that I hardly noticed that they left. As long as I could see the buck, I was immune to the cold and wind. After the deer dropped out of sight behind the ridge, however, time seemed to stop and I began to freeze. Their descent seemed to take forever, but soon we could see them scaling the far hill. The skiff of snow made climbing the steep slope dangerous, and they proceeded slowly—much too slowly for our liking.

Both Kirk and I had known from the start that the buck was far better than we led Dave to believe. Our consensus was that the buck was pushing 120 points and would probably be one of the top Coues bucks killed in Kirk's camps that season. The quality of the buck was reflected in our impatience while watching the three move up the distant slope. Finally, we had them lined up with an oak tree we had marked before the buck disappeared. Now it was up to them.

They advanced to the tree before they settled down to find the buck. We watched them glassing for one minute…two minutes…three minutes. I was about to go nuts. After 10 minutes, we were both pacing back and forth and wondering aloud why they couldn't find the

A collection of three great Coues deer bucks. From left: Jim Carmichel and Bill Hober.

buck. What had gone wrong? Maybe it had moved down the slope and on out of the canyon.

Our speculation died in the soft echo of a distant shot. We both sighed with relief when no second shot followed and we saw Jose' stand up. He was quickly joined by Alex and Dave. I was surprised, though, to see Dave turn and head back to the truck.

"Well, how big was he?" I asked when Dave arrived. "I don't know," he said, "José and Alex are bringing him around the crown of the hill. They didn't want to climb back up the ridge." Then he threw the question back at us, "How big do you think he is?"

"He'll score at least 105 points," Kirk said winking at me. When Alex and José arrived the cat was out of the bag. The "ohs" and "ahs" made Dave suspect that he had bagged a buck that wasn't just run of the mill. The fact that we couldn't quit talking about the buck and that every other sentence seemed to be punctuated with a *"muy grande"* confirmed his suspicions.

After dinner, we had two bucks to score, as Jim also stopped at the skinning shed with the buck he killed that afternoon. The final scores were both exciting and—for me—a little disappointing. Jim's buck green scored 110-6/8 points, while Dave's scored 117-3/8 points. Two great bucks brought to camp on the same day. That's a memory for a lifetime.

The disappointment came when both Tom and Kirk reminded me, several times, that once again I had earned "camp rat" honors. My only problem, I countered, was that Kirk had a "fetish for small bucks!"

Their good-hearted jabs aside, there is no way that I will ever be ashamed of a 106-point Coues deer buck. Still, I just hate the thought of putting up with their sarcastic jokes for 12 more months. I'll just have to get even with them next time. Maybe I should pray for snow on my next Coues deer hunt!

The Gray
Ghost
of Chihuahua

"THERE'S A BUCK!" I exclaimed. "Where?" asked my friend, Manuel Enriquez, owner of El Halcon Outfitters. I pointed toward a bench 600 yards uphill. Just then the buck broke into a trot, first feinting at a smaller buck and then chasing a lone doe through a small patch of oaks and over the ridge. It happened so fast that I got only a quick look at the diminutive whitetail's rack. The tines were tall, though, a good indication that he might be a high-scoring buck.

After describing what I saw, we decided to wait for at least an hour to let the deer bed down. It would be foolhardy to try a stalk with a buck and doe dashing all over the mountain, not to mention the smaller buck, which was also no longer in sight. It was late morning, and we guessed that the deer would be bedding soon.

Settling back, I swung my binoculars around to look into a basin we called the Honey Hole, because of the number of bucks we found there the previous year and the big buck I shot during that hunt. My glasses settled on a doe that was staring intently over her shoulder into the trees behind her. I watched to see what was holding her attention. Several minutes later, a buck stepped out with his nose to the ground, apparently scent-tracking the hot doe. When he saw her, he skidded to a halt and raised his head. That gave me a chance to see the rack, and it was instantly obvious that this buck deserved a much closer look.

While digging the spotting scope out of my pack, I whispered to Manuel that "a buck is walking across the rock slide in the Honey Hole." Manuel found the buck in his binoculars, took one look, and simply said, "Whew!", which accurately described the antlers that I was now looking at through my spotting scope.

We were well over one-half mile from the deer, yet its tines and main beams were clearly visible and impressive. Cooperating, the buck turned his head as he followed the progress of the doe nipping unseen morsels. The deer were moving slowly toward a dry creek bed, where it appeared they would drop out of sight, and we hurried to estimate the trophy potential of the rack. Manuel saw a small kicker coming off one of the G-2s that I didn't see, but we agreed the whitetail would score between 113 and 115 points, exceptionally large for a Coues buck. For 15 minutes we watched the big buck hound the doe before they eventually worked out of our sight. We waited for another half hour to make sure that they hadn't continued on out of the basin, then satisfied that the deer had bedded, we formulated our plan of attack.

We were headed to a small knob in the middle of the basin. It was familiar territory where Manuel and I had sat the year before and eventually killed a buck scoring 110 points. That buck had bedded just under the rim along the far basin wall within 200 yards as we sat on the knob. It would provide a perfect vantage point for us again. Once we got in position there were at least two possibilities. Ideally, we would spot the big buck bedded, allowing me a shot. The less desirable possibility was that we wouldn't be able to spot the buck in its bed and would have to wait until he got up and started feeding. That would mean a long wait on a hot day.

Between us and the knob was a free-standing rock fence that stretched from horizon to horizon. It was no Great Wall of China, which I've visited several times, but was nevertheless impressive. Built high enough to discourage the cattle and sturdy enough to survive the elements, it represented untold man-hours of back-breaking labor. With a base two- to four-feet wide and the top nearly the same, it was a formable obstacle; one that had cost me dearly the year before.

We picked our way carefully down the steep slope, trying hard not to fall into the clumps of cactus, crossed the rock wall, and

Manuel Enriquez evaluates the author's Coues buck just before the shot.

turned uphill toward the knob. Using the rocks in the crown of the knob for cover, we slipped off our packs and pulled out our glasses. We could see out to 400 yards and cover most of the likely hiding spots in the basin. The buck wasn't in sight.

Shortly after we got into position, hunting buddy Dick Jacobs and his guide, Carlos Terrazas, appeared in the distance on the south rim of the basin. After waving to acknowledge them, I was encouraged because they sat down and started glassing. Perhaps they had spotted the buck, as well. From time to time, I glassed them glassing us. We had water, lunches, and plenty of time. Good thing, because by evening all we had to show for our time was spotting a dozen or so does in groups of two to four. It was a long day.

Back at camp that evening, we found out that the buck hadn't bedded after all. Dick and Carlos explained that while we were climbing to the knob, they had watched "our" buck work his way up a side canyon and over the rim, passing within 200 yards of them. Dick had committed to killing a 120-class buck or go home empty-handed. This buck was big, he said, but he just watched the buck meander down into a canyon to the south. At first I was a little miffed that they had let us wait all day for a buck that wasn't even there. Carlos, however, later explained that they had assumed we were sitting on an even bigger buck.

Two big bucks had given us the slip, but ironically, both of those deer would later play pivotal roles in my hunt.

I first met Manuel at an SCI convention when I noticed a huge Coues deer rack on the floor of his booth. Before long, I was talking to Manuel and Carlos about their operation at El Halcon. Although they had conducted only a few deer hunts the previous year, both were long on hunting experience. Manuel and his father had hosted waterfowlers for years, building a solid reputation for

The little "gray ghost" can be tough to spot, especially when he beds tucked deep into cover.

results and service. They were also familiar with the Mexican regulations and paperwork that terrifies most alien hunters. Carlos had an outstanding Coues deer collection and years of experience hunting the little whitetails. They had my interest; leaving their booth I fully intended to return, but as shows sometimes go, I got busy. Several days later, Dick Jacobs ran into me on the convention floor and enthusiastically started to tell me about this promising new Coues deer outfitter he'd discovered. As you can expect, we returned and booked our hunt.

For years, I have hunted Coues deer in Sonora, but had never hunted in neighboring Chihuahua, although I had heard outstanding reports on the Coues deer hunting there. Dick had hunted in that state and was optimistic. On that first hunt we had been the only hunters in our camp, and what we found convinced me that El Halcon deserved to be on my "must do" list during my Deer Quest.

Manuel and Carlos often teased me with stories about a hidden basin to the west, where apparently many does bunched up during the rut. Bucks, including, I hoped, my big buck, would be drawn there as well. Unfortunately, to reach this mystery basin, we had to pass the Honey Hole, and in three attempts, we had never made it past the bucks we spotted there. Manuel suggested that in the morning we give it another try.

The trail up the ridge was beginning to show signs of our frequent climbs. When I finally topped out, my lungs felt like they were on fire. While I recovered, I couldn't help but stare at the spectacular sunrise reflecting crimson, yellow, and orange hues off broken clouds to the east. The electric colors glowed on the horizon in stark contrast to the deep blue, almost azure, of the sky above. Sunrises and sunsets are often spectacular bonuses for hunters in Mexico's desert mountains.

After the sun rose, we found plenty of deer, but none of them with the rack I was after. By mid-morning the weather had changed. It was blowing hard from the south, and the longer we sat and glassed the colder I got. At an altitude of 6,500 feet, dawn usually dictates a light coat that only a few hours later will be extra baggage;

however, we were still wearing our extra layers as we rose to continue toward the mystery basin. On our way, we decided to glass the other side of the ridge we were climbing, which was out of the wind.

At the first major ravine, we poked our heads over the rim and Manuel whispered, "There are two bucks and a doe!" The deer were right below us, less than 200 yards away. The rack on the biggest buck sported exceptionally high tines, and I guessed that he was the first buck that evaded us the day before. The other was a smaller 3 x 3. Ten minutes later we're still whispering to each other. I had the bigger buck pegged at 113 points, but Manuel was hesitant.

At 192 yards, from a dead rest over my pack, the shot was a "gimme." Before I got down to business, I remember thinking that the buck was a good deal larger than the doe beside it. The shot was anticlimactic, but at least it made one of the bucks happy. As we crossed the draw, the smaller buck rounded up the doe and herded her out of sight. When we approached the downed buck, I realized that I should have paid more attention to Manuel's instincts. I had no idea that "ground shrinkage" also affected the size of a buck's body, but the one lying there was a runt! I immediately realized that he was well short of the 113 points I had estimated.

At camp, the tape confirmed the "bad news." The rack green scored 106 points, matching the score of my Sonoran Coues. That's where the similarities ended! This buck had long tines, which was the only shortcoming of my Sonora rack. On the other hand, the Sonora buck had excellent mass and main beam length. If I could have taken the best features of both bucks, I would have had a heck of a "booner."

Just when I think I'm getting fairly good at field estimating, Mother Nature force feeds me a lesson in humility. Looking at the mount on my wall, most experienced hunters wouldn't question my field estimate of 113 points. The surprise comes when they are able to compare it to other nearby Coues mounts. Not only was the body deceivingly small, but the skull was almost three-quarter of an inch shorter than two others in camp.

I learned two lessons. First, trust the guide! Second, I have to be more careful of proportional scale. There were two reasons that my estimates were thrown off. The buck's tiny body made the rack appear larger than it really was in proportion to the head, ears, and muzzle. Each tine was approximately three-quarter of an inch shorter than my guesses, and I lost one- and one-half inches of mass on both sides. Still, the rack looks huge on the skull. I also suspect now that the doe I'd seen with this buck was a yearling.

T. R. White, holds his monster Coues deer killed in the author's "honey" hole. This buck evaded the author two days before, but thankfully returned. The buddy system was used to finally whack him.

Over the years, I've noticed more body-size variations in Coues deer than any other deer species. Big whitetails and mule deer are generally a lot larger than average bucks. With the smaller Coues whitetails, there is often only a difference of 25 to 35 pounds between a big and average deer. On future hunts I'll certainly pay more attention.

The author holds only one of many coyotes hammered while in Chihuahua.

My buck was down and my shooting was done, but there was still some hunting left to enjoy. Another hunter in camp, T.R. White, hadn't found a big buck yet, so that night over enchiladas we made our plans to be back in the Honey Hole at dawn. After a number of Coues deer hunts with other outfitters, he had yet to pull the trigger. The buck we found the day before would more than make up for those bad experiences.

Manuel must have had a premonition, because the next day he and I joined T.R. and his guide, Felipe "Turista" Chavez. Turista had been with Manuel and me on my first hunt with El Halcon when we killed my buck. I found that he not only had great eyes and was a pleasure to be around, but he was also a stud when the real work started.

We had been glassing from my favorite lookout for almost one-half hour when T.R. grunted, "There's a buck on the side of the basin!" It took several minutes for me to spot it standing near a doe in the mottled shade of trees. With his spotting scope, Manuel confirmed that it was the big buck. The deer had the advantage of elevation and would spot anyone trying a stalk from underneath. Getting within range might be tough. During the rut, it's almost impossible to predict how and when these sex-addled bucks will move. One minute a buck will be bedded, seemingly for the day, and in the next it's inexplicably beelining to some distant destination. Our ace in the hole was the doe. We were banking on her to hold the buck's attention until T.R. could get into position.

The commotion that would be created by four stalkers would be too risky, so Manuel and I stayed back to watch the show from the lookout. T.R. and Turista would circle to the west, cross two deep canyons, climb over the rock wall, and work up to the knob. From there they would be out of sight of the deer until they poked out in the rocks. It would give T.R. a shot of less than 300 yards—if the big buck stayed put. Only time would tell!

Shortly after the hunters dropped out of sight into the bowels of the first canyon, the buck started moving uphill, and my heart stopped. He seemed to be on a mission, and I had visions of him just continuing over the top just as he did when we spotted him a few days earlier. The big buck was halfway up the hill before I saw another buck, which, until then, had been hidden in some trees. What followed was worth the price of admission. The two bucks whipped all over the side of the mountain, but never got closer to each other than 20 yards. Finally, the biggest buck must have made his point, and the intruder retreated back into the trees. "Our" buck drifted back to the doe, which could have cared less. She was bedded under an oak tree and appeared to be asleep. The buck stopped on a small bench just above the doe before dropping into the grass for a well-deserved rest. Even though I had marked exactly where he was lying less than a yard away from a prominent rock, at times I swear he would just disappear. When I could make him out, however, it was clear that he was every bit as good as I thought when I first laid eyes on him.

We could see T.R. and Turista glassing from their vantage point, and I expected the echo of a shot at any moment. After what seemed like forever, we were getting concerned. Surely they could see him still lying in the grass. My blood pressure really spiked when the buck stood up. He was on the move again! I was beginning to panic when a shot rang out and the buck tumbled down the slope. Manuel and I both sighed with relief. We knew that T.R. had smoked a buck of a lifetime. I'll admit that when I saw the trophy tumble I had a flash of envy. I'm only human. It was the second hunt in a row that a hunting partner had killed a huge buck while I watched. The envy lasted only a moment before being overwhelmed by exhilaration as Manuel and I exchanged "high fives."

As happy as I was for T.R., though, I wasn't looking forward to the trip down the mountain or the climb up the small knob. The year before I had lacerated both of my Achilles tendons, and after a year of intense rehabilitation, walking on steep ground was still painful. I had also blown out my knee the year before while trying to climb over the rock wall while packing out my buck. That weakened knee was now my biggest problem. Now you know why that damn wall is painfully etched forever into my mind!

This time the wall didn't slow us down, the tendons held, and the knee didn't buckle when we scrambled over to check T.R.'s buck. The closer I got to the buck, the more convinced I was that our estimate was right on the money. I immediately put my tape on the buck where it lay in the grass. The rack rough scored at 115 SCI points. Later, I confirmed a score of 114-4/8 points. The accuracy of my long-range estimate somewhat renewed my faith in my field judging.

T.R.'s first Coues was a huge buck, but it wasn't the largest taken by El Halcon's clients. The top place was registered by a nontypical scoring an amazing 133-7/8 points. Five bucks were killed that scored 114 points or higher! As impressive as those statistics are, what impressed me most was that the first 15 bucks killed by El Halcon's clients, including the deer shot on our hunt, scored an average of 106-4/8 points. It would be difficult to duplicate that season's production of trophy bucks, although Manuel continues to try and is constantly adding promising ranches to his hunting area.

He has already secured the hunting rights to so much country that it boggles my mind. To give you an idea of the range available, Manuel and I took off from camp one morning long before light and headed for the most distant ranch in a complex of five ranches that we were hunting. We drove north for an hour before arriving at edge of the farthest ranch and it was another 20 minutes before we stepped out of the truck to start hunting. We were at an altitude of over 7,500 feet and into a mix of ponderosa pines and big oaks. The next day we traveled south over a half-hour to get to the other end of the complex into entirely different country and terrain.

If hunters could hunt every day of the season, I don't think they could cover all of the Coues deer country El Halcon has available. The vastness of this hunting area is one reason why I believe that Manuel's operation is capable of producing trophy Coues whitetails for years. As with other deer species, it takes a combination of age and genetics to produce big Coues deer bucks. El Halcon has both, which is why I look forward to returning to Chihuahua and again hunting with one of the rising stars in Coues deer outfitting.

I've already made Manuel promise to carry my ammo on my next trip and not let me load my rifle until we pass the temptations of the Honey Hole. Perhaps I will finally be able to nail one of those 120-class bucks!

Kirk Kelso watches Lechel's buck during the stalk. All this gear is gladly packed during a hunt because of the quality optics – an absolute necessity when hunting Coues deer.

Mike Schoby from Cabela's admires his fine whitetail taken with his muzzleloader the day before the author arrived in camp.

The Gap and its rocky cliff protect trophy whitetail deer in Wyoming. This is not your typical flat county most eastern hunters expect when they hunt out West.

Manuel Enriquez and the author spotted this Coues deer buck as it chased two does across a slope. Its high rack convinced them to return two days later for a closer look. Long tines and main beams made it impossible to pass.

Manuel Enriquez shows another way to pack a Coues
deer out whole. These little guys are a challenge
to hunt and live in remote and rugged country making
backpacking a necessity.

Only one of many food plots
available while hunting with
Eight Mile Outfitters. Notice how
shooting lanes have been cut
radiating away from the blind.

Mary Jones proudly shows the beautiful trophy Kansas whitetail she shot from her deck. Although two points were broken, this buck still scores over 166 points.

Hunting buddy, David Lechel, has a right to be smiling, holding a Coues deer buck like this one! Kirk Kelso and the author didn't even hesitate when this Sonora buck was first spotted, for obvious reasons.

A typical Coues deer habitat is rugged and rocky, making spotting one of the little whitetails difficult.

This is the way the author spends most of his time hunting. Top quality optics and a steady tripod are necessary to spot one of the diminutive Coues deer bucks in rugged country.

Just one more reason to love hunting Coues deer. Even a big buck can be packed out in one trip. José Valencia packed out the author's buck many miles using this technique.

Straight
Talk

Gear and Services

ONE ADVANTAGE of meeting other hunters in camp is that they often come from a wide variety of hunting backgrounds. I have found that their hunting experiences are a valuable source of information, since most hunters are more than happy to discuss their gear and why they selected it. I present this list and comments in that same spirit. It's only one man's opinion, but the equipment and services listed here work for me!

I'm constantly watching for a new gadget, or an adaptation of an old trick, to help me be a better hunter. The gear and services listed are what I used on my Deer Quest. This list evolved over four decades of hunting. It's always possible that a new piece of equipment may work better than what I'm already using, but just because it's new doesn't mean it's superior. Sometimes a new piece of equipment works better and sometimes it doesn't. In some cases, I've made improvements to factory equipment, and I've explained the changes. When a piece of equipment or service works better than what I'm using, I'll adopt it. I'm not on the staff of any equipment manufacturer, and I'm free to use the best equipment I can find.

I am also frequently asked for my packing list. The is my base list for a one-week hunt, and it can be changed as required for seasonal weather, duration of the hunt; whether I'll be housed in a tent camp, lodge, motel, or whatever; if I'm driving or flying; and finally, to meet weight restrictions.

BackPack   **Badlands**
                  1414 South 700 West
                  Salt Lake City, UT 84104
                  Tel: 800-269-1875
                  www.badlandspacks.com

My Model 2200 backpack was given to me by a friend, and it performs so well that I don't think that I will ever need another backpack. Its adjustable internal frame and suspension system makes this pack special, as it is very comfortable. Perhaps the best feature of the backpack is its full-length zippered opening in the back, something that I find that I am constantly using since it makes the contents of the pack readily accessible. My pack weighs 21 pounds loaded with the gear, binoculars and spotting scope that I often carry. I like the exterior tripod loops and open pocket for the tripod feet. It allows me to get to the tripod fast or easily pack it for a move. I have modified my pack by adding pockets, such as an extra binocular pocket added to the front of the pack. I have also added an interior pocket, made from netting for holding my water bottle upright.

Binoculars   **Swarovski Optik North America**
                  2 Slater Road
                  Cranston, RI 02920
                  Tel: 800-426-3089
                  www.swarovskioptik.com

I use the 15x56 WB binoculars whenever I expect to be glassing at long distance, such as on Coues deer or even many of my mule deer hunts. The optics are superior! These binoculars are easily carried in my pack in an exterior pocket that I had sewn on. Because of the magnification, these binoculars are best used with a sturdy tripod. I also purchased their 2X doubler for the binoculars, but found that it didn't produce the resolution I wanted. However, if I were on a backpack hunt, where every ounce counted, I would carry the doubler and these binoculars in place of my spotting scope.

Binoculars   **Leica Camera**
156 Ludlow Ave
Northvale, NJ 07647
Tel: 800-222-0118
www.leicacamera.com/sportoptics

I use the 10x50 BA Trinovids as my everyday binoculars of choice. While they are a little bulky and heavy, I gladly carry the extra weight because of the quality of the optics, besides my binocular straps distribute the weight effectively with no weight on my neck. These binoculars are extremely durable, and I've never had a problem with internal fogging. Their light gathering capability and resolution has made a difference for me seeing details under last-minute lighting conditions on a number of my hunts.

Binocular Strap   **Crooked Horn Outfitters**
26315 Trotter Dr.
Tehachapi, CA 93561
Tel: 877-722-5872
www.crookedhorn.com

I use the Bino-System because it allows me to carry my binoculars without weight directly on my neck. Also, their strap allows the binoculars to slide up when being used and then comfortably down when not. However, I modified their Bino-System by installing a quick-release buckle between my binoculars and the strap. I can quickly unsnap the binoculars and put them in my pack should I have to crawl.

Bipod   **Harris Engineering**
999 Broadway
Barlow, KY 42024
Tel: 270-334-3633

I use the Series S – 25 inch model to allow adjustment for canting while shooting. The legs can be extended so that I can shoot while sitting, if necessary, but still shoot from prone, which is the position I prefer. The legs can be adjusted to any height in their entire length, allowing compensation for a slope by adjusting one leg shorter than the other. I wish that they were lighter.

Boots   **Salomon**
5055 North Greeley Ave.
Portland, OR 97217
Tel: 800-225-6850
www.salomonsports.com

I have used the discontinued Authentic 8 leather boots for years and find them to be very comfortable. The replacement for this boot is the X Adventure 7 boot. I found the Authentic 8 to be extremely durable. The shank of the boot is relatively stiff and their Contragrip soles provide the necessary support and traction for crossing scree rock or where it is possible to turn or, worse, break a leg. These boots will also turn even the sharpest thorn, which is quite important when hunting in the desert.

Bullets   **Barnes Bullets**
PO Box 215
American Fork, UT 84003
Tel: 800-574-9200
www.barnesbullets.com

The 200-grain X bullet works very well in my .300 Remington Ultra Mag. With a BC of .550 and sectional density of .301, I find that it performs well in close or at long distance, yet I have shot sub three-inch groups at 500 yards. I used this bullet in Alaska because of the possibility of running into a bear. Since it is a copper-jacketed bullet, I find that it badly fowls my rifle. But, the extra time to clean the barrel is worth this bullet's performance. I moly coat these bullets.

Bullets   Swift Bullet Co.
                 PO Box 27
                 Quinter, KS 67752
                 Tel: 785-754-3959
                 www.swiftbullet.com

The 150-grain Scirocco bullet shoots very well in my 7mm magnum. The bullet has a BC of .515 and a sectional density of .266. It gives fine accuracy at ranges out to 600 yards, which is the farthest I have shot it. I killed seven of the eight bucks discussed in this book with this bullet. Five bullets were recovered. One retained 87% of its original weight, while the others ranged from 41% to 82% of their original weight. I was concerned about the results on the lower end. However, like the CEO of Swift pointed out, "You recovered them from a dead deer, didn't you?" This bullet also fowls my barrel, but I'll continue to use it because I haven't found another one that shoots better and still performs across a wide range of small-to medium-sized big game animals, such as from Coues deer to a bruiser mule deer.

Camera   Leica Camera
                 156 Ludlow Ave
                 Northvale, NJ 07647
                 Tel: 800-222-0118
                 www.leicacamera.com/sportoptics

I carry the Minilux compact camera in my pack. With this camera, I have taken award winning photos. The 40 mm F2.4 Summarit lens is superior. The camera uses aperture-priority auto exposure and generally delivers excellent results. While it doesn't have some of the gadgets and special modes that some other cameras have, over the last 10 years, it has never failed me. Certainly, it weighs less than many of the more complicated models.

Camera

Nikon
1300 Walt Whitman Rd.
Melville, NY 11747
Tel: 800-645-6687
www.nikonusa.com

This company's cameras have made their reputation by being used by some of the toughest critics – photojournalists. I have used the Nikon system as my bread-and-butter camera for years, but they are too heavy and bulky to carry in my pack. A variety of lens and filters, as well as my Nikon body is carried in a Halliburton case that has accompanied me on hundreds of trips worldwide.

Chronograph

Oehler Research
PO Box 9135
Austin, TX 78766
Tel: 800-531-5125
www.oehler-research.com

I have used the Model 35P Proof chronograph for years, and would not consider working up a load without it. The proof screen allows you to quickly determine if you have false velocity readings caused by poor lighting, glint, or a number of other causes. The unit has digital readouts, as well as a built-in printer, which allows me to keep a permanent record of high, low, spread, and mean velocities, and standard deviation data on my loads. I consider this equipment as a necessity in my handloading.

Clothing

Browning Arms
One Browning Place
Morgan, UT 84050
Tel: 800-782-4440
www.browning.com

I have used the Hydro-Fleece 4-in-1 parka under all kinds of weather conditions. It has never failed me even in Wyoming blizzards. The flexibility of layers is a powerful plus.

Clothing   CC Filson
                            PO Box 34020
                            Seattle, WA 98124
                            Tel: 800-624-0201
                            www.filson.com

I use the 17 oz. whipcord pant because it is lightweight, quiet, and durable—perfect for almost any fall hunt. The other pant is the Brush pant that I use where I expect thorns or heavy brush to be a problem. I also wear their lightweight wool shirts.

Clothing   King of the Mountain
                            2709 W Eisenhower Blvd.
                            Loveland, CO 80537
                            Tel: 970-962-9306
                            www.kingofthemountain.com

I use the Bushman wool shirts and Bunwarmer pants and often wear them without a coat during cold weather. Their clothing is very durable, yet it can be repaired. The only disadvantage is the weight and bulk while packing them for a hunt, but they are certainly warm when used with the correct undergarment.

Clothing   Predator
                            2605 Coulee Ave.
                            La Crosse, WI 54601
                            Tel: 608-787-0551
                            www.predatorcamo.com

I use the cotton shirts and pants during the early part of the season. This camo pattern seems to work under a wide variety of hunting conditions.

GPS   Garmen International
                            1200 E 151st St.
                            Olathe, KS 66062
                            Tel: 888-442-7646
                            www.garmin.com

I use the eTrex Summit because it is easy to use, and has the functions that I use most of the time in the field. This model is small. I never go on a trip without one.

Gun Case   **Mike Jacobsen Welding**
411 53rd Ave
Salem, OR 97304
Tel: 503-588-2957

My custom case was made with .063 gage aluminum and accommodates only one rifle. The gun case has three-inch heavy duty UHMW wheels. It also has a removable aluminum platform with pins that fit into holes in the case. Attached, the platform allows me to stack duffels and a camera case onto the gun case. Combined with a handle on the opposite end, I can use the case to wheel baggage about in an airport. Inside the case, an elastic net system is incorporated into the top of the case. After removing the foam padding, I place clothes compressed and packed in plastic bags in the top of the case and the net holds them in place. I also have tie-downs to prevent my rifle from slipping inside the case. Finally, four cam lock clamps with two separate locks discourage thieves.

Gunsmith   **Carolina Precision Rifles**
1200 Old Jackson Hwy
Jackson, SC 29831
Tel: 803-827-2069
CPRifles@aol.com

They provide accurizing work that any hunter, especially with a factory rifle, would do well to use. They will recrown the muzzle, pillar bed the action, float the barrel, lap the locking lugs, adjust the trigger, and lap the scope rings. It will cost $300 and is certain to improve the accuracy of most rifles.

Gunsmith   **Evolution**
PO Box 154
White Bird, ID 83554
Tel: 208-983-9208
www.evo-rifles.com

This company has done work on a number of rifles for me. I have never been dissatisfied with the end result; in most cases, it surpasses my hopes. They built my .300 Remington Ultra Mag and recently rebarreled my 7mm magnum.

Knife   **Kauffman Knives and Optics**
                        120 Clark Creek Loop
                        Clancy, MT 59634
                        Tel: 877-872-4264
                        www.hunttools.com

There are a number of outstanding knife makers in the US today, and Kauffman has to be included in almost any list. He made my sheath knife and a smaller caping knife to my specifications with ivory handles given to me by an African PH in the "old days." The knife is a work of art and keeps its edge through several skinning jobs. But, even when it does eventually get dull, the elephant leather sheath has a place for a ceramic, also capped with ivory. I carry it on every hunt except where governmental rules frown on ivory.

Laser Bore Sight   **Acu-Sight**
                        PO Box 1075
                        Mead, WA 99021
                        Tel: 888-777-8098
                        www.getontarget.net

This equipment is small and easy to pack in my duffel, but may well save a hunt. Despite the best of intentions, we can't always fire our rifles in camp to confirm zero. With a laser bore sight, you can do this in limited space or at night without ever firing a shot. I learned a lesson while on my Utah trip and will never leave home again without the proper laser bore sight for my rifle

Moly Coating   **Neco**
                        536 C Stone Rd.
                        Benicia, CA 94510
                        Tel: 707-747-0897
                        www.neconos.com

This company provides moly coating services, as well as other products for shooters. I find that their coating service is not only inexpensive, but eliminates the mess associated with doing it myself. You send them your bullets and they return the coated bullets quickly. They deal in batches of 24,500 grains (slightly over three boxes of 150 grain bullets).

Muzzleloader   Modern Muzzleloading
                    PO Box 130
                    Centerville, IA 52544
                    Tel: 641-856-2626
                    www.knightrifles.com

I have used two Knight in-line rifles made by this company. Currently, I use the stainless .50 caliber Disc rifle. The other rifle that I use is the MK-85. I am constantly amazed how accurately these rifles shoot. This company also provides a full line of accessories.

Powder   Hodgdon Powder
                    6231 Robinson
                    Shawnee Mission, KS 66202
                    Tel: 913-362-9455
                    www.hodgdon.com

I have used this company's powder in many of my rifles, from the centerfire to my muzzleloaders. Their Extreme family of powders is less influenced by ambient temperature which makes bullet velocities more consistent from early fall to late winter. Their Pyrodex pellets are my first choice for my muzzleloader, when it is allowed in the state I am hunting.

Rangefinder   Leica Camera
                    156 Ludlow Ave
                    Northvale, NJ 07647
                    Tel: 800-222-0118
                    www.leicacamera.com/sportoptics

I use the LRF 800 Rangemaster. This unit can be carried in my shirt pocket, keeping the batteries warm and the rangefinder accessible. The diopter allows compensation adjustment for each person's eyes. I am considering upgrading to their LRP 1200 Rangemaster because it has a stronger laser and is more accurate in unfavorable conditions. However, if money, size and weight were not an issue, I would use their Geovid model because it will give readings when other rangefinders fail.

Reticle Changes   **Premier Reticles**
175 Commonwealth Court
Winchester, VA 22602
Tel: 540-868-2044
www.premierreticles.com

This company performs reticle work on Leupold scopes. You can send them the trajectory of your pet load, and they will add mil-dots, additional strata lines, or a wide selection of reticles. I have strata lines added to my Leupold scope set for 400, 500 and 600 yards, and they have served me well in many hunting situations.

Rifle Scope   **Leupold & Stevens**
PO Box 688
Beaverton, OR 97075
Tel: 503-526-1400
www.leupold.com

I use the 6.5-20 x 50mm Long Range scope for almost all my hunting, except where I will be hunting thick brush. Admittedly, the 6.5 power is not ideal for close running shots. I have used this scope for my hunting and silhouette shooting for so many years, I am very comfortable using it. The focus adjustment on the side of the scope is very handy.

Scope Cover   **Michaels of Oregon**
PO Box 1690
Oregon City, OR 97045
Tel: 800-948-1356
www.uncle-mikes.com

I use the clear Blizzard scope cover because it uses "optical grade" polymers, allowing the most complete transmission of all see-thru covers. This cover provides a waterproof seal in all types of weather. The spring-up covers can be used closed in the event that a quick shot is required, or raised for a long-range shot.

Sling Swivels   **Boonie Packer Products**
PO Box 12517
Salem, OR 97309
Tel: 800-477-3244
www.Booniepacker.com

I use this company's Safari Swivel because it has a safety pin pre-
venting it from opening by accident, yet is not difficult to install.
This feature will prevent the swivel from opening while carrying a
rifle saving a damaged rifle, scope or ruined hunt. I have never had
a problem with these swivels.

Sling   **Michaels of Oregon**
PO Box 1690
Oregon City, OR 97045
Tel: 800-948-1356
www.uncle-mikes.com

I use their Quick-Adjust sling. I don't use a sling in the traditional shooting manner, so I have little need for the military-type
sling. In most cases, I am shooting from prone across a pack or from
my bipod. I do, however, use the sling to safely carry my rifle. The
sling I use is made from nylon webbing and is very strong, yet light.
It does have a keeper in the event that I must use a hasty sling.

Spotting Scope   **Nikon**
1300 Walt Whitman Rd.
Melville, NY 11747
Tel: 800-645-6687
www.nikonusa.com

I have used the 78 mm ED Field Scope for the last several years.
The ED glass is not only difficult to get, it is expensive. But the
quality is extremely high. I also purchased their 20-45x eyepiece
allowing me to use the power ranges most frequently needed in the
field. If I would change anything, I would probably buy the 60 mm
ED glass in this same model, because it is smaller, lighter, less
expensive, and has a sliding sunshade.

Taxidermy   Madison Range Taxidermy
509 MT Hwy 287 N #9
Ennis, MT 59729
Tel: 406-682-7405
www.mrtbiggame.com

Ike Reed has done my taxidermy work for the last 20 years. Although he charges a competitive price for his work, he is not a production taxidermist, meaning that he takes the time to do the little things that makes a mount "come to life." He will also take the time to deal with the small details that make a big difference in the quality of the mount. He not only does extremely high quality work, but he does it quickly—often, within a few months after the trophy is sent to him. He enters a number of taxidermy competitions nationwide and places well in the Masters class. Recently, he won two blue ribbons in the Open Division for whitetails at nationals, possibly the toughest taxidermy competition in the USA.

Tripod   **THK Photo Products**
2360 Mira Mar Ave.
Long Beach, CA 90815
Tel: 800-421-1141
www.thkphoto.com

I use the Slik 444-Sport II tripod because I feel it offers the best compromise of weight, adjustment height, and rigidity for hunting. The three-section legs allow the tripod to be compacted for carrying on my pack, yet extended for use while standing. The center post has a geared elevator that I find handy. The legs are fully adjustable to adapt to almost any terrain. Because it doesn't have the internal braces between legs found on some other tripods, I can place the Slik strattling my legs and comfortably glass while sitting. I have other heavier tripods I use for my photography work, but this tripod goes with me on my hunting trips. I have replaced the original tripod head.

Tripod Head   **Uni-Daptor**
3597 East Pine Cone Dr.
Williams, AZ 86046
Tel: 928-635-5316
wjimjack@aol.com

I use the Uni-Daptor tripod head because it is lightweight, yet rugged. The head is also very smooth and the adjustments are positive. When adjusted properly, I can move my binoculars on the tripod smoothly to follow a feeding animal. It is also small, allowing me to leave the head attached to my tripod while carrying them on my pack. In addition, they provide two types of quick-release plates that I find invaluable to attach to my binoculars or camera.

Packing List
5-Day hunt, Mild Conditions

Wear During Travel:
- ☐ Salomon Boots
- ☐ Socks
- ☐ Underwear
- ☐ Short Sleeve Shirt
- ☐ Pants & Belt
- ☐ Money and Credit Cards
- ☐ Handkerchief
- ☐ Hunting Cap
- ☐ Watch

Flightbag:
- ☐ Leica Camera
- ☐ Leica 10 x 50 Binoculars
- ☐ Swarovski 15 x 56 Binoculars
- ☐ Garmen GPS
- ☐ Leica Rangefinder
- ☐ Spiral Notebook & Pencil
- ☐ Glasses and Sunglasses
- ☐ Flight Tickets
- ☐ Licenses and Permits
- ☐ Recorder and Tapes

Extra Clothes:
- ☐ 3 Pair Light Socks
- ☐ 2 Pair Medium Socks
- ☐ 5 Sets Underwear
- ☐ 2 Long Sleeve Hunting Shirts
- ☐ 2 Camouflage Shirts
- ☐ Filson Pants
- ☐ Orange Hunting Vest
- ☐ Camp Slippers
- ☐ Fleece Vest
- ☐ Light Gloves
- ☐ Browning Jacket Liner

Miscellaneous:
- ☐ Gun Case
- ☐ Rifle, Scope, Sling & Bipod
- ☐ 30 Rounds Ammo
- ☐ Slik Tripod
- ☐ Nikon Spotting Scope
- ☐ Canvas Duffel Bag
- ☐ Small Towel
- ☐ Dobber Kit
- ☐ Crazy Creek Chair
- ☐ Dirty Clothes Mesh Bag
- ☐ Garden Hose Pieces
- ☐ Cape Sack
- ☐ Badlands Pack
- ☐ Rain Gear
- ☐ Water Bottle
- ☐ Extra Boot Liners
- ☐ Measuring Packet and Tape
- ☐ Maps
- ☐ Sleeping Bag with Cover
- ☐ Pillow
- ☐ Small Flashlight and Batteries
- ☐ 2 Rolls Fiber and Duct Tape
- ☐ Kauffman Knives
- ☐ Chalk Bottle
- ☐ First Aid and Emergency Kit
- ☐ Space Blanket
- ☐ Rope
- ☐ Rifle Kit
- ☐ Belt Cartridge Case
- ☐ Acu-Sight Unit

Camera Case:
- ☐ Camera, Flash & Lenses
- ☐ Film

Appendix

Outfitters,
Guides
and the Like

Outfitters:

German Rivas De La Torre
Rancho El Carbon
Saratoga 236 Casa 8
Naucalpan, Edo., Mexico, C. P. 53900
Tel: 011525552901500
E-mail: cazamayor@prodigy.net.mx

This outfitter offers desert mule deer and Coues deer hunts in
Sonora, Mexico.

Jim & TinaMarie Schaafsma
Arrow Five Outfitters
Star RT 1 Box 64A, Zenia, CA 95595
Tel: 707-923-9633
E-mail: arrow5@cwnet.com

This outfitter offers Columbia blacktail and pig hunts in northern
California. In addition, they offer Coues deer hunts in Mexico.

Kim Bonnett & Jeff Warren
Bucks & Bulls Guides & Outfitters
270 North Main, Lindon, UT 84042
Tel: 801-785-5050
E-mail: bucksandbulls@bucksandbulls.com

This outfitter offers mule deer and Rocky Mountain elk hunts in
Utah. In addition, they offer antel:ope hunts in northeastern
New Mexico and Utah.

Kirk & Roxane Kelso
Pusch Ridge Outfitters
11077 E Escalante Rd., Tucson, AZ 85730
Tel: 520-544-0954
E-mail: kirkkelso59@aol.com

This outfitter offers Coues deer, sheep, antelope, and elk hunts in Arizona; antelope hunts in New Mexico; whitetail hunts in Kansas; and sheep, mule deer and Coues deer hunts in Mexico.

Manuel Enriquez
El Halcon
1650 Sioux Dr, El Paso, TX 79925
Tel: 888-603-4322
E-mail: mxhunter@hotmail.com

This outfitter offers Coues deer and mule deer hunts in Chihuahua, Mexico.

Mary & Stan Jones
Eight Mile Outfitters
11255 SW 200th St., Douglas, KS 67039
Tel: 316-747-2494
E-mail: emoinc@earthlink.net

This outfitter offers whitetail hunts in Kansas. They are represented by Associated Hunting Consultants as a booking agent.

Mike Watkins
Trophies Plus
PO Box 44, Alzada, MT 59311
Tel: 800-248-6899
E-mail: trophiesplus@rangeweb.net

This outfitter offers mule deer and whitetail hunts in the southeast corner of Montana, the northwest corner of South Dakota, and Wyoming. They also are represented by Jim McCarthy Adventures as a booking agent.

Oscar Molina
San Jose Trophy Hunts
Escobedo No 42 Col. Inalambrica, Hermosillo, Sonora, Mexico
Tel: 011526622143056
E-mail: ormolina@hmo.megared.net.mx

This outfitter offers mule deer and Coues deer hunts in Sonora, Mexico. His United States representative is The Trophy Connection.

Wayne Long
Multiple Use Managers
PO Box 669, Los Molinos, CA 96055
Tel: 800-557-7087
E-mail: mum@volcano.net

This outfitter offers hunts for mule deer, Columbia blacktail, and pig hunts in California, as well as Sitka blacktail, black bear and reindeer hunts in Alaska.

Booking Agents:

Cliff Graham
Associated Hunting Consultants
6593 Mars Road, Cranberry Twp., PA 16066
Tel: 724-772-4868
E-mail: cliff@hunts.net

This booking agent represents Eight Mile Outfitters.

Jim McCarthy
Jim McCarthy Adventures
4906 Creek Dr, Harrisburg, PA 17112
Tel: 717-652-4374
E-mail: jmcarthy@epix.net

This booking agent represents Trophies Plus.

Kurt Hughes, The Trophy Connection
PO Box 2565, Cody, WY 82414
Tel: 800-308-1161
E-mail: info@thetrophyconnection.com

This booking agent represents San Jose Trophy Hunts in the United States.

Miscellaneous:

Boone & Crockett Club
250 Station Drive, Missoula, MT 59801
Tel: 406-542-1888
E-mail: bcclub@boone-crockett.org

Pope & Young Club
PO Box 548, Chatfield, MN 55923
Tel: 507-867-4144
E-mail: pyclub@isc.net

Safari Club International
4800 West Gates Pass Road, Tucson, AZ 85745
Tel: 602-620-1220
E-mail: rbrown@safariclub.org

The Hunting Report
9300 S Dadeland Blvd Suite 605, Miami, FL 33156
Tel: 800-272-5656
E-mail: mail@huntingreport.com

Adfognak Native Corporation
215 Mission Road, Suite 212, Kodiak, AK 99615-1277
Tel: 907-486-6014
E-mail: www.adfognak.com

The Adfognak Native Corporation allows hunting on their lands for a variety of game species with permits.

The Last
Word

T HERE YOU HAVE IT! More than a year has passed since the first hunt in my Deer Quest. I have just finished the first drafts of this book and stopped to reflect back on my adventures. My quest took several precious months out of my life as I traveled over 20,000 miles in pursuit of my dream. At the end, I had a tremendous sense of accomplishment. However, I also felt a need to share the fantastic deer hunting we enjoy here in North America with other hunters. You'll see why in a few moments!

When I was a young boy, my grandfather and I would race each other to the mailbox where, if we were lucky, we would find the latest edition of *Outdoor Life*, *Field & Stream*, or *True* magazines. This was so long ago that most of you won't even remember that *True* was originally a great outdoors magazine. Authors of the ilk of Grancel Fitz plied their trade there, thrilling us "wannabes" with their stories of captivating adventures. We dreamed of experiencing those adventures ourselves.

The stories those authors spun helped create a generation of hunters with a thirst for adventure and a need to experience hunting in the far reaches of this earth. Many sportsmen and wildlife personnel today can trace their love for the outdoors, at least in part, to those early writers. They touched us not only by what they wrote, but also by the hunting legacy they left behind. For example, Fitz, in his 1947 article in *True* magazine, coined the term "Grand Slam" and changed the course of sheep hunting forever. In short, those old-time authors captured our interest and fired our imagination.

Writers, in those days, were good storytellers and prided themselves on their ability to spin a tale, to convey the emotions and the essence of their adventures so that readers could live their hunts vicariously. Through Russell, Ruark, O'Connor, Page, and others, we could imagine ourselves freezing on some bare face of talus rock slope waiting for that big buck to emerge from the trees below. We lived our dreams through their writings. In those articles there was no concerted effort to convey the science of the hunt—that is, the how-to and where-to information, the nuts and bolts, if you will. Instead, the art of the hunt carried the message, and the science was entwined in the story, not as the main theme, but as a subplot. The old-timers hunted to experience the subtle rewards of the hunt, not simply to kill.

In my early writing career, I was fortunate to have received guidance from mentors such as Jack O'Connor, Warren Page, and P.O. Ackley. I soon learned that my writing allowed me to enjoy my hunts even more because I was able to relive them and dwell on the satisfactions, the trials and tribulations, as well as the emotions and heartaches hunting produces. It's all a part of the hunting experience and one of the subtle things many hunters miss today. Consider that many hunts in the old days were packtrain trips scheduled for weeks at a time, allowing plenty of time to enjoy the wonders of wildlife and the outdoors. Contrast that with many hunts today where often the success of the hunt is measured in its short duration.

Warren Page once told me that experience was the great teacher. I took that to heart and dedicated myself to the hunt—to live each hunt as if it were my last. As the winter of my hunting career draws to a close, I wanted to once more write as we did in the old days. I wanted to convey the adventure of my Deer Quest. My hope is that it will fire the imagination of a few of my readers to follow in my footsteps. Along the way, I have tried to share the hunting techniques and gear that I use. Perhaps that will be of help to my readers in their hunts, but, once again, that wasn't the focus of this book.

Whether it is a whitetail hunt in your backyard or a mule deer trip in Sonora, hunting deer is a challenge. It's that challenge that drives me. I have always thought that the more difficult the challenge, the more satisfying the reward. In that vein, I undertook my Deer Quest. The scores were only a means to an end! My biggest fear is that some readers will assume that this book was all about killing deer simply for entry into one of the various record books.

That assumption would be wrong...Life is too short—get out and do some hunting! —Lance Stapleton

About the Author

Aᴜᴛʜᴏʀ, writer, publisher, photographer, and worldwide sports-man, Lance Stapleton is no stranger to the hunting fraternity. Born and raised in the Colorado Rockies, he spent his early years outdoors. After graduating with a master's degree in business, he spent much of his professional career until retirement in the transportation and telecommunications industries.

In parallel, his writing career spanned 40 years. Stapleton's byline appears regularly in major national and regional publications. He has authored two previous books, *A Reference Manual for Hunting North American Sheep* and *Trophy Mule Deer*. Both were written with a strong emphasis on where to hunt and were loaded with comprehensive information about the respective species.

Stapleton resides with his wife, Sally, in Oregon's Willamette Valley. He is a member of the Outdoor Writers Association of America, a life member of the Foundation for North American Wild Sheep and Mule Deer Foundation, and is a proud member of the NRA and Safari Club International, as well as a number of other sportsmen's and conservation organizations.